TRAILBLAZING GROWTH

A FINANCIAL ADVISOR'S GUIDE TO LEADING CLIENTS ON A JOURNEY OF CLARITY, CONFIDENCE, AND TRUST

JOEL CRAMPTON

TRAILBLAZING GROWTH
A Financial Advisor's Guide to Leading Clients on a Journey of Clarity, Confidence, and Trust

COPYRIGHT © 2026 Joel Crampton
Published by CMO Alpha Publishing

ISBN:
979-8-9943864-0-8 *Paperback*
979-8-9943864-1-5 *Hardcover*
979-8-9943864-2-2 *eBook*
979-8-9943864-3-9 *Audiobook*

~ For Cooper and Colin ~
May you blaze your own paths to success.

CONTENTS

Mapping the Client Journey i

Introduction ii

How to Use This Book vi

Your Prospect Is Already Halfway Down the Trail 1

Why Firms Are Stuck in "Random Acts of Marketing" 13

The 8 Critical Stages of a High-Value Client Journey 25

Stage 1 – AWARENESS
The First Spark of the Journey 43

Stage 2 – EXPLORATION
Why Prospects Wander, Loop, and Drift 55

Stage 3 – EVALUATION
Where Confidence Begins and Trust Finds Its Footing 75

Stage 4 – CONVERSION
The Moment a Prospect Hands You Their Gear 95

Stage 5 – ONBOARDING
Building Trust and Momentum 111

Stage 6 – SERVICING
Delivering Ongoing Value Clients Feel, Not Just See 127

Stage 7 – LOYALTY
The Long Miles Where Trust Deepens and Relationships Last ... 143

Stage 8 – ADVOCACY
When Clients Become Ambassadors for Your Firm 155

Conclusion 169

Acknowledgments 176

About the Author 178

MAPPING THE CLIENT JOURNEY

Every successful advisory relationship follows a journey.
But before we start walking the trail, it helps to see the map.

The framework below maps the eight stages clients move
through as they progress from uncertainty to clarity, from
hesitation to confidence, and ultimately to deep, enduring trust.

Throughout this book, we'll return to these stages repeatedly,
exploring what clients need at each moment, and reveal how the
most effective firms intentionally design strategies that earn trust
and drive growth.

The 8 Stages Of Trailblazing Growth

Benefit	Goal Achieved In The Journey	Stage Focus
Clarity	The client understands their problem and the solution.	Awareness Exploration Evaluation
Confidence	The client commits to the solution and feels secure in their choice.	Conversion Onboarding
Trust	The client feels valued, well-cared for, and becomes a promoter of your firm.	Servicing Loyalty Advocacy

With this map in mind, let's begin the journey...

INTRODUCTION

Every important journey in life begins long before you realize you've stepped onto the trail.

That truth hit me years ago on the Inca Trail in Peru — a four-day hike in the Andes mountains, through thin air and ancient stone that tested every part of me I thought was strong. The path was steep, the altitude was real, and every step forced me to confront the difference between what I thought I could carry and what I actually could.

But what made the experience possible wasn't my legs or lungs. It was the porters.

They moved with a quiet confidence that seemed impossible at that altitude. While the rest of us fought for breath, they ran ahead with our packs, set up camp, and created a sense of certainty in a place where everything else felt uncertain. They didn't walk the trail for us, they simply made it possible for us to keep going.

That feeling has stayed with me for years. Because whether you're climbing a mountain or running a firm, the deepest truth is the same: No one succeeds alone. Everyone needs a guide somewhere along the way.

Your prospective clients feel this long before they ever call you. They sit in quiet moments, sometimes at their kitchen table, sometimes in the car, sometimes at the edge of their bed, and think:

"Am I missing something?"
"Are we going to be okay?"
"Should I be doing more?"
"Is this the right path?"

They wrestle with uncertainty, comparison, guilt, pride, and responsibility. They wonder if they're behind. They try to organize the pieces: the accounts, the spreadsheets, the advice from friends, the articles they've saved, the plans that no longer match their current life.

Before they ever step into your office, they are already deep into their own journey, one they've been walking alone.

Most advisors don't see this. Not because they don't care. But because the industry has never really taught them to look.

Traditionally, "marketing" meant campaigns, funnels, ads, mailers, workshops… anything that pushed people toward a meeting. But that framework completely ignores the emotional and psychological reality of how real people make real decisions about something as personal and vulnerable as their finances.

People don't move through funnels. They move through inner terrain. They seek clarity before they seek help. They observe before they engage. They evaluate silently before revealing themselves. They walk far before asking for a guide.

When you look closely at this inner terrain, you discover something else: every prospective client moves through three emotional milestones long before they become a client.

First, they search for Clarity — a way to make sense of their situation and see their path more clearly.

Then they look for Confidence — reassurance that the decisions they're making are sound and that the person guiding them is trustworthy.

Finally, they seek Trust — a felt sense that they are seen, supported, and safe moving forward.

Clarity. Confidence. Trust.

These are the emotional anchors of the client journey, and everything an advisor says, builds, or delivers either strengthens or weakens them. The chapters ahead will show you how each stage of the journey aligns to one of these outcomes and how small, intentional actions can help clients move forward long before they ever sit across from you in a meeting.

This book is about that unseen path.

It's about understanding the real journey your prospective clients take, the one that begins months or years before they ever appear in your CRM, and learning how to build a marketing and growth system that meets them where they already are.

Not with pressure. Not with noise. Not with "look at me" tactics. But with relevance, resonance, and rhythm.

Because growth isn't something you bolt onto your business, it's something you unlock when you truly understand the people you serve.

Over the coming chapters, you'll explore the stages a prospect travels as they move from initial awareness to becoming an engaged, loyal, and referring client. You'll see why most firms lose people in the early quiet stages, and how simple shifts in messaging, structure, and experience can create exponential improvements in trust, conversion, and long-term growth.

You'll also see yourself inside this journey. The decisions you make about growth within your firm follow the same psychological arc your clients follow.

Because advisors walk their own trail, full of moments of hesitation, overwhelmingness, second-guessing, bursts of clarity, and stretches of effort that don't seem to move the needle. The better you understand both journeys — yours and your clients — the more confidently you can lead.

And leadership, in both journeys, always begins with clarity, builds through confidence, and matures into trust.

You don't need to overhaul everything. You just need a clearer path, one that helps prospective clients move forward easier. A path that helps your firm stay aligned. A path that helps you avoid carrying more than you should.

The journey has already begun for the people looking for someone like you. They're halfway down the trail, deciding which guide to follow.

Growth accelerates when you guide that journey with intention, and this book will help you meet them where they are on their journey.

HOW TO USE THIS BOOK

This book is designed to be practical, not theoretical. Every chapter follows a consistent rhythm, so you always know how to apply what you're learning inside your own firm.

Think of it as both a field guide and a strategy manual, something you can read straight through or reference whenever you need clarity on a specific stage of the client journey.

As you move through each stage, you'll notice that the client journey follows a deeper emotional pattern. Early stages help prospects gain clarity, middle stages strengthen confidence, and the later stages cultivate long-term trust. These emotional outcomes anchor every chapter, and the tools you'll find inside are designed to help you support clients through each one with intention.

They also form the foundation of sustainable growth because firms grow fastest when clarity, confidence, and trust compound across every stage of the journey.

To help you put these ideas into action, each chapter ends with three quick-hit sections:

Trail TIPS

These are simple, practical prompts you can use with prospects or internal team members. They help you translate the chapter's ideas into real conversations, decisions, or actions that support both better client experiences and better growth strategies.

Trail MARKERS

These checkpoints confirm whether your firm is aligned with how modern clients make decisions. Use them as a self-assessment. If a marker feels off, that's a sign of where your next improvement lies and where your growth may be stalling without you realizing it.

TRAILBLAZING GROWTH

This section shows how I help advisors apply the concepts in real engagements. Think of it as a window into how a fractional marketing leader operationalizes the journey inside a firm. It connects the theory to actual practice so you can see how intentional experience design translates into measurable growth.

🥾 Look Out For Boot Marks

Throughout the chapters, you'll see a small boot-mark icon. Whenever it appears, it signals an immediate action step, something you can implement quickly to strengthen a specific part of your marketing or client experience.

These are meant to be simple, high-leverage moves you can make without needing a full strategic rebuild — small steps that often create disproportionate growth when layered consistently over time.

My goal is to give you a structure that meets you where you are and moves with you as your firm grows. You'll find ideas you can implement today, insights that strengthen your long-term strategy, and simple cues that help you guide clients toward clarity, confidence, and trust.

Because when you elevate the client journey, growth isn't something you chase, it becomes the natural outcome of how you show up.

However you choose to use this book, let it support you the same way great guides support their travelers — quietly, consistently, and at exactly the moment you need it.

Your Prospect Is Already Halfway Down The Trail

"People decide long before they act.
The best leaders pay attention to the moments
that cannot be measured."
– Peter Drucker

Prospective clients are on a financial journey you will never see in its entirety. They don't begin it when they fill out your contact form or walk into your office. They begin long before that, in quiet, private moments when uncertainty interrupts their normal routines.

Research across the financial and consumer sectors consistently shows that prospects complete a majority of their decision-making before ever contacting a firm. This invisible stretch isn't just a psychological stage, it's where the seeds of your firm's growth are planted.

It might start at the kitchen table, where stacks of statements feel heavier than they used to. It might start after a conversation with a spouse that ends with more questions than answers. It might start when a parent falls ill, or when market volatility rattles their sense of security, or when they realize that "someday" planning has quietly turned into "now".

These early moments don't feel like a journey. They feel like tension building inside a life that's already full.

But these moments are the journey, and they shape everything that follows.

Most advisors don't see it. Not because they aren't paying attention, but because the industry has conditioned them to believe the journey starts only when a prospect becomes visible.

The truth is the opposite.

The Journey Starts Before You're Aware Of It

Modern prospects complete most of their evaluation before they ever talk to a human being. Edelman's Trust Barometer found that 59% of buyers prefer to make decisions independently before contacting a professional.

In other words, by the time someone reaches out to you, the emotional groundwork has already been poured. And your growth depends on how well your firm shows up during this hidden evaluation period.

They've researched quietly. They've compared options. They've tried to make sense of their financial picture on their own. They've built private narratives around what they fear and what they hope is still possible.

Their eventual outreach is not the starting line, it's a checkpoint. Whether they reach that checkpoint with you or with someone else is determined long before you ever know they exist.

Why People Don't Move In Straight Lines Anymore

For years, firms relied on the classic "marketing funnel" — awareness at the top, decision at the bottom. But funnels don't reflect how humans make decisions today.

McKinsey's consumer research shows that only 13% of people follow a linear buying path anymore. Instead, people loop, wander, bounce between platforms, and revisit information multiple times before moving forward. They advance when something gives them clarity, and they retreat when something raises doubt.

Growth accelerates when your firm supports this looping behavior instead of trying to force people down a straight path.

The journey is emotional before it's logical. Internal before external. Private before public.

Prospects don't want to talk until they're nearly sure. They want to feel oriented before they feel exposed.

Your marketing either supports that process or silently pushes them away.

The Digital First Impression

The first "meeting" between you and a prospective client doesn't happen in your office. It happens through what I call the Digital First Impression stack — the collection of online signals that shape how someone perceives your firm long before they engage.

This stack includes:
- Your Google search results
- Your website (especially the About, Process, and Philosophy pages)
- Your LinkedIn and social media presence
- Your articles, insights, and educational content
- Photos and tone
- Reviews and testimonials
- And increasingly, AI-generated summaries of your firm scraped from your digital footprint

Deloitte reports that the average American now consumes 11.8 hours of digital content per day, and financial content is one of the fastest-growing segments. Prospects aren't just "checking you out", they're evaluating:

Do these people understand someone like me?
Do I feel safe with their tone and approach?
Does this advisor speak with clarity OR complexity?
Does this firm feel modern, dated, or disconnected?

If your digital presence feels scattered, generic, or confusing, prospects will quietly eliminate you, without ever telling you that you were being considered.

The earliest part of the client journey is invisible, but decisive. The quality of your Digital First Impression is one of the strongest early predictors of growth.

The Desire For Autonomy

Pew Research found that 81% of Americans prefer to do their own research before making major decisions. This desire for control is even more pronounced in financial matters, where fear, identity, and vulnerability collide.

Prospects want to understand you before they reveal themselves to you. They want to gather enough context to feel prepared. They want the emotional safety of evaluating from a distance.

They are not avoiding advisors; they are protecting themselves. Your growth depends on your ability to create an environment that feels safe enough for autonomy-driven prospects to take the next step.

By the time they make contact, they've already carried the emotional weight of this journey on their own shoulders for far too long.

Referrals Follow The Same Path

Even referrals behave this way. A friend or colleague might recommend you, but the referred prospect still Googles your firm, reads your bio, explores your content, and forms their own impressions before engaging. The referral encourages outreach, but the prospect still needs conviction to act.

This is why so many advisors notice referral volatility. Referrals no longer "skip" the journey. They simply skip the first few steps. And firms that understand this process convert referrals at far higher rates.

Advisors Walk A Similar Journey

Here's the part most advisors don't expect: You behave exactly the way your clients do.

Clients try to DIY their finances until they feel overwhelmed. Advisors try to DIY their marketing until they feel overwhelmed.

Clients consume information from everywhere but still feel confused. Advisors consume marketing advice from everywhere but still feel unsure.

Clients hesitate to reach out to a guide. Advisors hesitate to hire strategic marketing leadership.

Neither behavior is irrational. Both are deeply human.

Your growth challenges mirror your clients' financial challenges, and understanding that parallel gives you compassion for both journeys.

The Invisible Early Journey

The earliest part of the client journey (the part you never see) is where:
- emotional tension builds
- uncertainty forms
- preferences develop
- trust begins
- stories take root
- decisions quietly shift
- competitors are eliminated

It's invisible, but it's everything.

When you understand this stage, your marketing shifts from feeling like a push, to becoming a guidepost. You stop trying to "get attention" and instead begin building a trail that reduces fear, clarifies meaning, and creates momentum.

This is the foundation of modern growth. Most firms overlook it. The firms that master it grow with far less friction and far more consistency.

What prospects are really searching for in this early, invisible stretch is clarity — clarity about their situation, their options, their risks, and their possible future.

Before someone can feel confident enough to reach out or trust enough to engage, they must first make sense of what they're experiencing.

This chapter begins the first of those emotional shifts. The coming sections will show how clarity becomes the foundation that confidence and trust are eventually built upon.

Marketing Is The Trail That Brings Prospective Clients To You

Marketing is not a set of campaigns. It isn't a collection of tactics. It isn't a funnel. Marketing is the trail that brings someone from uncertainty to clarity, from isolation to support, from confusion to confidence.

It's the connective tissue between:
- what prospects feel
- what they hope
- what they fear
- what they need
- and the moment they finally reach out

Your role is not to push people forward. Your role is to guide them long before you meet them.

Guides don't create the journey, they illuminate it. They help people see more clearly, move more confidently, and ultimately feel safe enough to trust the path ahead.

That progression — clarity, confidence, trust — is the emotional architecture of every client relationship you'll build. And when you reinforce that architecture intentionally, growth becomes a natural outcome of how you show up, not a separate project you chase.

It all begins here, long before the first conversation.

Trail TIPS
Conversation Prompts For Halfway-Down-The-Trail Prospects

By the time prospects reach out, they've already done a significant amount of emotional and informational work. These prompts help you meet them where they truly are, not at the beginning of the journey, but deep into their private decision-making process.

They also help you create conversations that naturally increase engagement and strengthen the conditions for healthy, sustainable firm growth. Ask your prospects these questions:

What led you to start exploring your options recently?

What have you already researched on your own?

When did this start feeling important to address?

What questions or concerns came up as you explored?

What would help you feel confident taking the next step forward?

9

Trail MARKERS
Understanding Today's Modern Prospect

Use these checkpoints to confirm alignment with how modern prospects make decisions and ensure your firm shows up in a way that supports their real-world evaluation process.

When these markers are strong, your early-stage pipeline becomes warmer, more qualified, and more consistent — a key driver of long-term growth.

- ☐ I understand that prospects complete most of their evaluation before contacting us.
- ☐ My brand look-and-feel shows up consistently across social media, search (Google, AI, etc.), and our website.
- ☐ Our digital presence tells a clear, coherent story prospects can follow independently.
- ☐ We create content that prospects can consume on their own time.
- ☐ Visitors can easily understand who we help and how we help them.

TRAILBLAZING GROWTH
How I Support Advisors At This Stage

At this early stage of the client journey, most firms underestimate how much prospects have already researched and decided before the first meeting.

My role is to illuminate that hidden stretch of the trail. I strengthen the digital first impression, clarify the narrative prospects encounter, and remove the friction that keeps them from moving forward with confidence.

This work directly supports growth by increasing the volume of right-fit inquiries and reducing the lag time between initial interest and first contact.

This is where early gaps in the client experience surface. We map the unseen beginning of the journey, refine the Digital First Impression Stack, and align messaging with the questions prospects are already asking.

When your early-stage presence is clear, consistent, and confidence-building, your firm enters more prospect conversations already ahead.

The result is a pipeline with warmer leads, higher conversion potential, and a growth engine fueled by clarity rather than complexity.

When this foundation is solid, inquiries become warmer, conversations flow more naturally, and trust begins forming long before anyone sits down for a meeting.

Why Firms Are Stuck In "Random Acts Of Marketing"

"If you don't know where you are going,
you'll end up somewhere else."
– Yogi Berra

Every advisory firm reaches a point where marketing feels heavy. The team is active. The calendar is full. New ideas pop up constantly. And yet... results feel unpredictable and disconnected.

Growth is happening, but it feels accidental, fragile, and impossible to predict.

This is the signature feeling of "Random Acts of Marketing" (RAM). RAM is not caused by laziness or apathy. It's caused by effort without direction. It's what happens when a firm wants to grow but has no shared map for how growth is actually created.

The Drift Into Randomness

RAM almost never arrives suddenly. It creeps in slowly, disguised as productivity. Someone updates the homepage. Someone else posts on LinkedIn. An advisor records videos. A workshop gets planned. A new trend gets chased.

Individually, these moves make sense and feel rational in the moment. However, together they create a fragmented, inconsistent marketing environment. The team becomes busy but not coordinated. Over time, these uncoordinated actions stall growth, even as everyone feels busier than ever.

The Emotional Cost Of Disconnected Activity

On the surface, RAM looks tactical. Underneath, it drains confidence. Leaders start asking:
"Are we doing the right things?"
"Why aren't we seeing more traction?"
"Are we missing something?"

Uncertainty breeds reactivity:
- chasing new ideas out of fear
- pivoting too quickly
- experimenting without clarity

Deloitte found that 32% of executives cite marketing uncertainty as a major barrier to growth. In advisory firms, the percentage is even higher due to compliance pressure and complex decision cycles.

RAM isn't chaos. It's uncertainty masquerading as activity. Inside the firm, clarity erodes first, then confidence, and eventually trust in the marketing itself. When that happens, leaders pull back on investment, hesitate to commit to long-term initiatives, and unintentionally slow their own growth.

How Firms Wander Off The Trail

Most firms drift into RAM gradually. Small detours and quick fixes add up, pulling the team off a clear path.

The reasons are understandable:
- rapid growth
- unclear brand messaging
- inconsistent advisor communication
- outdated website structure
- shifting compliance constraints
- too many tools, not enough integration

But these are surface-level factors. The real roots run deeper. Each small detour absorbs capacity that could be building a repeatable growth engine.

Why Firms Fall Into Random Acts Of Marketing

Financial services leaders rarely choose chaos. It accumulates slowly for any number of reasons. Over time, a few recurring obstacles keep showing up and pulling firms off course. The main ones are:

1. **They believe they already understand marketing.**
   Principals are natural problem-solvers. They assume marketing should be solvable through effort alone. But subject-matter expertise does not automatically translate into brand-building expertise.

   What works to grow client assets one-to-one does not automatically scale to one-to-many.

2. They've been burned before.

Most advisors have had a bad vendor experience. Once trust is broken, they retreat into DIY mode — even if they're not equipped to run a modern marketing function. Growth becomes something they "try" between client meetings rather than something they lead intentionally.

3. Compliance creates friction.

Compliance is essential but it creates psychological resistance. J.D. Power reports 45% of advisors cite compliance as their biggest marketing challenge, causing many to default back to referrals-only even when they want growth. The result is a firm that says it wants to grow but operates as if growth is too risky to pursue consistently.

4. They hire junior help and expect senior-level strategy.

A young marketer is hired to "do everything" without clear leadership or structure. They were hired to execute tasks not build a strategy. Tactics multiply, but a cohesive growth plan never emerges.

5. They copy competitors without context.

If a competitor's video gets attention, the firm copies it. If a peer launches a guide, everyone wants a guide. This is mimicry, not marketing. Copying tactics without understanding the underlying strategy rarely produces the same growth outcome.

6. They confuse activity with progress.

A webinar here. A mailer there. A few posts. It feels like momentum, but without a cohesive strategy, activity doesn't build anything meaningful. Energy is spent, but there is no clear connection between what the firm is doing and how it will predictably create new ideal-client relationships.

What RAM Looks Like In Reality

RAM shows up as:
- inconsistent posting
- scattered messaging
- unclear value proposition
- content aimed at "everyone"
- siloed advisor communication
- tools that don't integrate
- metrics tracked without context

Eventually, someone says: *"We're doing a lot… but nothing feels connected."* That's the hallmark of RAM. It's growth by accident instead of growth by design.

Fragmentation Is The Real Enemy

RAM's biggest cost isn't money, it's fragmentation. Your website says one thing. Your advisors say another. Your content sounds different from your delivery. Your ads don't match your messaging. And prospects become confused.

McKinsey found that companies with strong internal alignment grow revenue 36% faster than those without it.

Why? Because aligned systems compound. Fragmented systems cancel themselves out. Fragmentation makes the entire firm feel heavier than it needs to be. From a growth perspective, fragmentation acts like a tax on every new initiative — you work harder for smaller returns.

The Hidden Cost Of RAM

RAM doesn't just exhaust your team; it erodes trust long before you ever see the results. Here's what RAM really costs an advisory firm:

1. **Decision Fatigue**
    Leaders spend more time evaluating new ideas than executing proven ones.

2. **Internal Confusion**
    Messaging shifts. Priorities move. No one knows the story.

3. **Brand Dilution**
    Inconsistency causes mental strain for prospects, and trust begins to decline.

4. **Missed Compounding**
    Great marketing compounds; RAM resets the clock.

5. **Lower Conversion Rates**
    Friction pushes prospects away without them knowing why.

6. **Advisor Fatigue**
    Constant reinvention wears people out.

7. **Slower AUM Growth**
    The real cost isn't money; it's the opportunities lost.

Over years, these costs quietly cap the firm's growth potential, even when the team is talented and the client work is excellent.

Why Effort Without Strategy Creates Burnout

Marketing without structure is like hiking without a map. You can work hard, sweat, put in the hours... and still feel like you're not moving. Burnout occurs when:

- wins feel accidental
- failures feel personal
- new ideas feel like resets
- no one knows which effort matters
- nothing compounds

The problem isn't the work, it's the randomness. When effort is no longer clearly tied to progress, people begin to doubt whether growth is even possible.

Why Strategy — Not More Activity — Ends The Chaos

When firms are stuck in RAM, they often look for a new campaign, a new tool, a new channel, a new content idea. But tactics don't fix fragmentation. They amplify it.

A real strategy gives a firm:

- direction
- clarity
- consistency
- integration
- measurable progress
- confidence

Inside the firm, strategy restores clarity and confidence. Outside the firm, it creates a coherent experience that clients can trust.

Cerulli reports that firms with a defined client experience grow 2–2.5x faster than those without one. In other words, a clear, intentional client journey is a growth strategy, not just a service philosophy. The firms that grow are not doing more. They are doing the right things in the right order.

And that's the shift this book teaches. Once a firm steps out of randomness and onto a clear path, everything becomes easier — decisions, marketing, communication, and client experience.

Strategy restores traction. It puts every effort to work. It turns scattered activity into a journey that feels clear, builds confidence, and earns trust. When that happens, growth stops feeling like a gamble and starts behaving like the natural result of how you operate.

Now let's walk that journey, one stage at a time.

Trail TIPS
Evaluating Random Acts Of Marketing

Before a firm can build a clear strategy, it has to see where randomness still shapes decisions. Use these prompts to slow down, assess current activity honestly, and spot where effort lacks direction or connection. They also help you identify which efforts truly drive growth, and which simply keep you busy.

Which of our activities actually support the client journey?

Where does our message feel inconsistent or unclear?

What are we doing out of habit rather than strategy?

Where are prospects experiencing friction?

Which activities reliably lead to right-fit conversations and new clients, and which rarely move opportunities forward?

Trail MARKERS
Identifying RAM Inside Your Firm

Use these checkpoints to spot early signs of Random Acts of Marketing and to confirm whether your firm's efforts are supporting a single, cohesive journey rather than a disconnected set of tasks. When these markers are strong, your marketing becomes a true growth system instead of a collection of one-off experiments.

- ☐ Our marketing activities connect into a unified system.
- ☐ Our messaging is consistent across all platforms.
- ☐ We no longer "start over" with each new idea.
- ☐ Our tactics support a clear client experience.
- ☐ Our team understands the purpose of each activity.
- ☐ We can connect key activities to specific stages of the client journey and to measurable growth outcomes.

TRAILBLAZING GROWTH
How I Support Advisors At This Stage

Most firms don't need more activity. They need a leader who can create structure, remove friction, and replace randomness with clarity so growth can become predictable instead of accidental.

This is the inflection point where I step in as the strategic anchor, the person who sees the full landscape, connects the dots, and rebuilds marketing as a system instead of a series of disconnected tasks.

RAM becomes obvious the moment we map the client journey end-to-end. Advisors can instantly see where messaging drifts, where digital touchpoints break the story, and where effort is being wasted. We then reallocate energy toward fewer, higher-impact initiatives that directly support pipeline health and AUM growth.

From there, I unify the narrative, redesign the digital presence, and rebuild the marketing rhythm around how modern clients actually make decisions.

We define clear priorities, establish simple scorecards, and make it easy for the team to see how their work contributes to growth.

The result is focus, confidence, and growth that compounds — not because the firm is doing more, but because everything finally works together.

THE 8 CRITICAL STAGES OF A HIGH-VALUE CLIENT JOURNEY

"When dealing with people, remember you are not dealing with creatures of logic, but with creatures of emotion."
– Dale Carnegie

Every client moves through the same psychological stages before they ever become a loyal advocate. Some move quickly. Some move slowly. Some walk the trail confidently; others hesitate at every turn. But the pattern is always there, and when you understand this pattern, growth stops feeling unpredictable and starts becoming intentional.

The challenge is that most firms only recognize the middle of the journey — meetings, paperwork, onboarding, reviews. They see the visible part of the trail. But the most important steps happen long before the first conversation.

If you want sustainable, predictable growth, you must understand the full arc of how clients actually make decisions. This journey is rarely linear and always emotional.

That emotional journey follows a remarkably consistent pattern. Early stages help prospective clients gain clarity — clarity about their situation, their options, and the decisions ahead. Middle stages build confidence, as clients begin committing to the path and experiencing your guidance for the first time. And the later stages deepen trust, the feeling that they are understood, supported, and safe moving forward.

Clarity, confidence, and trust are the emotional anchors of the entire client journey, and each stage reinforces one of them.

They're also the anchors of business growth. When clarity breaks down, growth stalls. When confidence rises, conversion rises. When trust compounds, referrals compound.

Traditional marketing terms feel too clinical in a high-trust profession. They don't reflect the emotional experience that drives someone to hire a financial advisor... or the internal experience that leads an advisor to hire marketing help.

A more accurate lens is discovery and guidance. Clients aren't sliding through a funnel. They're walking a trail, interacting with fears, hopes, expectations, and uncertainty. They're looking for someone they trust enough to guide them.

Seeing The Journey From Both Sides

There are always two journeys happening at once — the client's journey and the firm's journey. Most advisors only see the client side, but your marketing decisions (and who you choose to lead them) follow the same emotional arc — hesitation, curiosity, evaluation, commitment.

Clients ask: *Can I trust this advisor with my future?*
Advisors ask: *Can I trust this marketing path with my brand?*

Clients ask: *Do I feel understood?*
Advisors ask: *Do they understand my niche, my compliance needs, my growth goals?*

Clients ask: *Is this the right guide?*
Advisors ask: *Is this the right strategy? The right partner? The right timing?*

When you see both journeys clearly, everything becomes easier. You design experiences that create clarity early, build confidence through action, and strengthen trust over time. You design experiences that support clients and systems that support your team. You reduce emotional bottlenecks. You build processes that match how humans actually make decisions.

A firm that understands both journeys makes better marketing choices, grows more intentionally, and creates a client experience strong enough to sustain growth long after the initial touchpoint.

This chapter outlines the eight stages of the modern journey. You will see your clients in these stages. And you will also see yourself. Because the journey they walk is not that different from the journey you walk in your own business. Both journeys move through clarity, confidence, and ultimately trust, whether you're choosing a guide or becoming one.

Stage 1: Awareness

Every journey begins with a moment of awareness. For clients, it often sounds like this:

"I don't feel confident about retirement."
"I think I'm missing something with taxes."
"I wonder if I'm making the right financial choices."
"My accounts are scattered and I have no real plan."

Sometimes it's a dramatic moment; more often it's subtle, a quiet sense that something is off. Clients usually start here long before they take action.

The Financial Planning Standards Board reports that 67% of people delay seeking financial advice until a major life event forces the issue. That delay is why Awareness is emotionally charged: clients aren't just solving a problem, they're confronting avoidance.

Awareness is the hiking equivalent of thinking, *"It might be time for an adventure."* No trail chosen. No gear purchased. Just a pull towards change.

Advisors experience this same stage in their marketing:
"Our growth is inconsistent."
"Our marketing is scattered."
"We can't keep doing this ourselves."
"We need someone who understands this."

Awareness isn't a decision, it's realization. A spark of momentum that fades unless supported by clear next steps.

For firms, this is often the moment when growth aspirations begin to crystallize, the point where *"we wish we were growing faster"* becomes *"We need a better path."*

To be clear, this Awareness stage is likely different from what you're used to hearing in traditional marketing conversations.

In most frameworks, awareness means awareness of YOU — your firm, your brand, your services. But that's not how real journeys begin, especially in high-trust decisions like financial planning. People don't wake up thinking, "*I need an advisor.*" They wake up sensing that something has shifted. A growing complexity. A quiet discomfort. A feeling that what once worked may no longer be enough.

Awareness, in this journey, isn't about discovering a firm. It's about recognizing a gap between where someone is and where they want to be. It's the moment a person pauses and thinks, "*Something here deserves attention.*" Only after that awareness takes shape does the search for guidance begin.

Stage 2: Exploration

Once the spark forms, people begin exploring. Curiosity increases. Options multiply. Clients gather information to understand what they're facing... and in financial services, the number of options can feel overwhelming.

Clients explore by:
- comparing different types of advisors
- asking friends or other professionals for referrals
- searching online
- browsing advisor websites
- reviewing credentials
- reading articles or watching videos
- consulting AI tools for clarity

They're trying to understand the landscape — who does what, why it matters, and who feels trustworthy.

Google found that 89% of consumers begin their buying journey with online research, even for high-trust services. This means prospects evaluate you long before you know you're on their radar.

Advisors mirror this stage when evaluating marketing help, by asking themselves if they should:

- DIY their marketing
- do nothing
- hire an agency
- hire an in-house marketer
- hire a fractional leader
- rely solely on referrals for growth

Exploration is powerful but exhausting. When everything is an option, it becomes harder to identify the right one.

Exploration is also where many growth opportunities are quietly lost, not because the firm lacks ability, but because prospects cannot yet understand the firm's value.

Stage 3: Evaluation

This is where the real decision-making begins. Clients narrow their list and move from *"What are my options?"* to *"Which option feels trustworthy?"*

Evaluation includes deeper questions such as:
Do they understand people like me?
Do they solve my problems?

Do I like how they communicate?
Does their philosophy align with how I think?
Do they seem consistent and competent?

This is where your content matters most — articles, podcasts, videos, newsletters, emails, and social posts. Prospects study your consistency, clarity, and tone.

Evaluation is choosing your hiking guide — comparing routes, understanding the approach, and deciding whose leadership feels right. It's not just skill-based; it's trust-based.

Edelman's Trust Barometer research shows trust is now the #1 factor in decision-making, above price, convenience, or product features. When a firm communicates clearly and consistently across channels, it becomes the "safe path" in the prospect's mind.

Evaluation is also the stage where nurturing becomes essential. Prospective clients often linger here, especially in high-trust industries like financial planning. It's common for someone to follow an advisor's content for months before reaching out.

Advisors evaluating marketing support ask similar questions of their potential marketing partner:
Do they understand financial services?
Have they walked this path before?
Can they handle compliance?
Do they understand advisor growth?
Do they feel like someone I can trust?

Evaluation is thoughtful and slow, which is why nurturing matters. It's also where growth pipelines strengthen or leak. Firms that nurture consistently grow faster, not because they push harder, but because they stay present while others disappear.

Stage 4: Conversion

Conversion happens the moment a commitment is made, when someone says, *"I'm ready. Let's do this."*

In financial services, this often looks like:
- agreeing to the planning fee
- signing paperwork
- transferring accounts

But conversion isn't the end; it's the beginning of a shared journey. It's stepping onto the trail with your guide.

Vanguard's Advisor Client Study found that clients choose advisors primarily because they feel understood, not due to performance or technical details. When prospects sense alignment, the emotional burden drops and commitment becomes easier.

Advisors feel this same relief when choosing a marketing partner. Once committed, direction becomes clearer and focus increases.

Conversion turns intention into momentum. From a growth perspective, it's where pipeline becomes revenue and where clarity and confidence pay off.

Stage 5: Onboarding

Onboarding is one of the most fragile stages. This is where trust is either confirmed or shaken. It's the client's first real experience with your systems, communication, and support.

If onboarding goes well, confidence skyrockets. If it goes poorly, doubt creeps in.

Clients want to feel:
- they made the right choice
- they are understood
- the process is smooth
- their advisor is organized
- their questions matter
- they are not alone on the trail

Onboarding is the first mile of the hike, where the client determines whether they're comfortable with your pace and leadership. Strong onboarding accelerates future growth by improving retention, increasing referrals, and reducing early-stage uncertainty.

Stage 6: Servicing

Servicing is where the relationship settles into rhythm. It's steady, ongoing, and foundational. This is where consistency either strengthens confidence or slowly erodes it.

Clients want to feel supported, informed, guided proactively, remembered, and valued.

Proactive reviews, planning updates, reminders, and thoughtful outreach reinforce trust. When servicing is weak or inconsistent, uncertainty grows... and loyalty fades.

Servicing prepares clients for the final stages of the journey. It's also the stage where firms quietly lose or gain lifetime value — the core economic engine of growth.

Stage 7: Loyalty

Loyalty is not created by performance alone; it's created through consistency. J.D. Power found that 1/3 of clients leave their advisor because of poor communication, not results.

Loyalty happens when a client feels:
- understood
- supported
- informed
- appreciated
- valued

Loyalty is reinforced at every touchpoint. It grows through the small moments that make clients think, *"This is why I chose them."*

Loyal clients stay longer, deepen relationships, and stabilize growth, creating the foundation that Advocacy later amplifies.

Stage 8: Advocacy

Advocacy is the summit. It's when clients carry your reputation into rooms you've never entered. Advocacy isn't about asking for referrals, it's about earning them.

Advocacy looks like:
- enthusiastic recommendations
- warm introductions
- sharing their experience
- becoming a true promoter

It's the hiking equivalent of returning from an incredible journey and telling others, *"You have to do this — with this guide!"*

Advocacy is the most powerful growth force in a trust-based profession — and the least understood. When trust compounds, referrals become natural, not forced.

A Simple Journey Scorecard

Before you move on to the stage-by-stage chapters, use this quick scorecard to assess how well your firm supports each part of the journey. Think of it as a snapshot of where you are today. No firm scores perfectly. The goal is simply to identify where your strengths already shine and where small improvements could create a far better experience for prospects and clients.

This clarity will make the upcoming chapters even more actionable. Rate each of the following statements as:
1 = Strong, 2 = Developing, or 3 = Needs Work

Journey Stages   Score

1. Awareness
My firm helps prospects articulate their concerns, not just react to inquiries.

2. Exploration
Our digital presence answers the questions prospects are quietly asking.

3. Evaluation
We demonstrate clarity, competence, and consistency across all touchpoints.

4. Conversion
We remove friction and make the first commitment feel calm and confident.

5. Onboarding
Our systems and communication reinforce trust within the first 90 days.

6. Servicing
Our ongoing experience is proactive, predictable, and personal.

7. Loyalty
We maintain a clear communication rhythm that builds long-term confidence.

8. Advocacy
We earn referrals naturally by delivering a memorable, meaningful experience.

Your scorecard tells you where your journey is strongest and where small improvements will create major impact.

High-Trust Journeys Require More Care

Financial services is a high-trust industry. They're handing over their life savings, plans, anxieties, and hopes.

High-trust journeys require:
- more nurturing
- more clarity
- more consistency
- more communication
- more reassurance

Low-trust purchases happen quickly. High-trust decisions happen when emotional safety is present. You can't rush these steps; you can only guide them.

Your Clients Are Walking This Journey. So Are You.

Clients move through the eight stages. Advisors do, too. Which is why firms that understand this journey outperform those that don't. They aren't guessing, they're guiding. They aren't improvising, they're intentional.

Once you understand these stages, your entire strategy shifts. Marketing stops being a list of disconnected efforts and becomes a structured, human-centered journey.

This is the map. The next chapters show you how to walk it with clarity, build confidence at every step, and earn trust that lasts.

Trail TIPS
Reflection Questions For Your 8-Stage Journey

Now that you have a clear map of the eight stages, these prompts help you reflect on how well your current experience matches the journey your clients are actually walking.

Where do our clients feel the most friction or confusion?

Which stages are we supporting intentionally, and which are happening by accident?

Where do we tend to lose people in the journey, and why?

Which stage, if improved even slightly, would create the biggest downstream impact?

Do we have at least one clear process, message, or touchpoint for each stage?

Which stage currently limits our growth the most and what simple improvement would create momentum?

Trail MARKERS
Mapping The 8 Stages Clearly

These checkpoints confirm your firm understands the full journey and that you're beginning to see your marketing and client experience through the lens of all eight stages.

- ☐ We have processes, messaging, or content supporting each stage.
- ☐ I can identify when someone moves from one stage to the next.
- ☐ We avoid skipping stages or rushing prospects.
- ☐ We recognize that prospects move at different speeds and with different needs.
- ☐ My firm reviews our journey map at least annually.
- ☐ We can link each stage to key growth outcomes (conversion, retention, referrals).

TRAILBLAZING GROWTH
How I Support Advisors At This Stage

Most advisors don't need more ideas. They need clarity, structure, and a system that turns intention into consistent execution. My role is to translate the 8-stage framework into something practical — a blueprint the firm can actually run, measure, and improve over time.

We define what each stage looks like inside the firm, mapping it to real touchpoints, processes, and milestones.

Your team gains a shared understanding of what "good" looks like from Awareness through Advocacy.

We also connect each stage to measurable growth outcomes — stronger inquiries, warmer conversions, healthier retention, and more natural referrals — so the entire journey becomes a growth engine rather than a loose philosophy.

Together, we turn a compelling framework into the operating system for your marketing and client experience, so growth becomes intentional, repeatable, and far easier to manage.

STAGE 1

AWARENESS:

THE FIRST SPARK OF THE JOURNEY

*"Change happens when the pain of staying the same
is greater than the pain of change."*
– Tony Robbins

Emotional Outcome: **Clarity**

Awareness is the moment clients begin making sense of their
situation, long before they take action. Your role is to offer
clarity without pressure, so more of the right people begin
moving toward you instead of staying stuck in silence.

Every journey begins with a moment of truth — the instant something inside us shifts. A moment when we realize the way things are is no longer the way things can stay. For your future clients, that moment is Awareness, the quiet spark that eventually leads them to your door.

Awareness is not action. It's not commitment. It's not even a decision. It's the internal realization that something is off, missing, or no longer sustainable.

Think about your own moment of Awareness. The point when you knew you couldn't keep doing the same thing. Maybe that was when you chose to start your business, build an independent brand, realized referrals alone would not support the next stage of growth, or stopped relying on chance for new clients.

For most prospective clients, Awareness happens long before they become aware of your firm. They feel uncertainty and friction, a gap between where they are and where they want to be. Awareness is the mind reaching for clarity, even when the person isn't ready to act. They may not have the vocabulary to articulate it yet, but they feel it.

Here's what Awareness often sounds like:
> *"I feel behind on retirement."*
> *"I think I'm making decisions without understanding the consequences."*
> *"I'm guessing too much with taxes."*
> *"Our financial life feels scattered."*
> *"I'm not confident we're doing this right."*

Awareness rarely arrives in one dramatic moment. It comes from small, consistent signals — a friend's comment, a tax bill, a market drop, an unexpected expense. These micro-realizations accumulate until the emotional weight becomes too loud to ignore.

The Quiet Moments That Spark Change

Most moments of Awareness don't feel urgent at first. A client checks their portfolio during volatility and feels anxious. They overhear someone mention a planning strategy they've never considered. They search "how much do I need to retire" and end up more confused.

These small moments stack until they reach a threshold. That's the true beginning of the journey — not a single event, but the buildup of many quiet ones. Clarity doesn't arrive all at once; it forms slowly, as small signals begin connecting into a larger truth.

Why Awareness Feels So Heavy

Awareness feels heavier in financial planning because it collides with behavioral biases:

- **Regret aversion** – fear of discovering they should've acted sooner
- **Status quo bias** – clinging to familiar patterns even if they're ineffective
- **Complexity avoidance** – delaying action when next steps feel unclear
- **Identity conflict** – money touches beliefs, hopes, and self-worth

Clients don't suddenly proclaim, *"I need help."* They reach a tipping point.

When The Idea First Appears

For me, Awareness is the stage I was in long before stepping foot on the Inca Trail. I felt a pull toward adventure — no gear purchased, no research done, no training started. Just the awareness that something new was calling.

Every meaningful journey begins this way: not with action, but with possibility.

Your clients have this same moment long before they contact you. And advisors experience the same moment with their marketing.

Clients Aren't The Only Ones Who Feel This

Just as clients experience discomfort and uncertainty, advisors do too — especially around marketing.

Advisor awareness sounds like:
"Our growth is inconsistent."
"We have no real marketing plan."
"This is taking too much of my time."
"I'm doing random acts of marketing."
"We need someone who understands this."
"I can't keep carrying this alone."

Awareness is when leaders finally realize and admit something has to change. They've felt the strain of disjointed marketing and the fatigue of trying to do it all themselves. It's also the point where the desire to "grow better" starts to outweigh the temptation to keep improvising.

Advisor Blind Spots During Awareness

Advisors often rationalize away their own discomfort:
> *"This is just a busy season."*
> *"We'll fix the website later."*
> *"We'll market more when we hire someone."*
> *"We'll get to it next quarter."*

But the tension remains. Awareness isn't weakness, it's strategic realization.

Awareness Is A Psychological Trigger

This stage marks the shift from complacency to curiosity. People move from ignoring something to acknowledging it. But awareness is fragile. Most people don't act. They sit in the discomfort. They rationalize it away. Real life intervenes.

People hate losing progress, emotionally or financially. Loss aversion is strong enough that prospects cling to familiar but ineffective paths because the fear of choosing the wrong advisor outweighs the hope of choosing the right one.

Awareness needs support, a catalyst for action.

My father, a psychologist, often told me people rarely change until the discomfort of staying the same exceeds the fear of doing something different. In financial planning, we want to intercept people long before their situation becomes a crisis. Awareness shouldn't be rock bottom.

But clarity alone isn't enough. It must feel safe before someone is willing to move toward it. It should be the moment a person recognizes a better path is available.

Why Most Prospects Stay Stuck Here

Awareness creates emotional friction because acknowledging a need means acknowledging vulnerability. Prospects fear:
- being judged
- appearing uninformed
- exposing financial mistakes
- being pressured
- making a wrong choice

Advisors who understand these emotional blocks create environments where prospects feel safe, and safety creates movement. The more often you provide that feeling of safety at this stage, the larger and healthier your future pipeline becomes.

Awareness Creates Questions

Clients rarely ask these questions out loud, but they feel them:
"Where do I begin?"
"What type of advisor do I need?"
"What if I make the wrong choice?"
"Who can I trust?"
"What will this cost me?"
"How do I know who is actually good?"

Advisors experience their own version:
"Who can I trust with our brand?"
"What does a good strategy look like?"
"What if I hire the wrong person?"
"How do I know who really understands our industry?"

This book helps both sides understand the map.

Awareness Begins Long Before You Know It

By the time a prospect visits your website or follows you on LinkedIn, they've spent months — sometimes years — in the Awareness stage. By the time they book a meeting, the emotional decision is already underway.

Awareness is invisible but foundational. It looks like silence from the outside. It feels like uncertainty on the inside.

And it's happening constantly — for both clients and advisors.

The Role Of The Firm During Awareness

The firm's job at this stage is simple:
Be discoverable.
Be clear.
Be reassuring.

People in the Awareness stage aren't ready for a pitch. They're looking for gentler signals:
- clarity of purpose
- simple messaging
- steadiness
- relief from complexity

Your brand should whisper, *"You're not alone. We help people like you every day."* When your presence does this well, Awareness turns from a private struggle into the starting line for future growth.

What Prospects Look For Without Realizing It

At this stage, people subconsciously look for three things:
- **Emotional safety** – *"Will I feel judged?"*
- **Predictability** – *"Will this feel chaotic or structured?"*
- **Identity alignment** – *"Are these my kind of people?"*

Before prospects compare performance, they compare emotional signals.

Awareness Is The Beginning Of Trust

A client's Awareness moment is when trust-building begins. Everything they see afterward influences whether they choose you.

You can't control when Awareness happens. But you can control the world prospects step into once it does.

Two Paths — Healthy Vs. Crisis Awareness

There are two types of Awareness:
- **Healthy Awareness** – early realization, openness, curiosity
- **Crisis Awareness** – something breaks… death, divorce, taxes, market shock, business sale

Firms that support both paths with empathy win.

The Journey Never Starts At Zero

Prospects have already walked internal miles before contacting you. They've researched, worried, compared, and hesitated.

You meet them halfway.

Advisors feel the same when they finally decide to get serious about marketing.

Awareness Creates Momentum For Stage Two

Awareness leads naturally into Exploration, the mental shift that follows the emotional one.

The next chapter shows how prospects navigate to the next stage (Exploration) and what firms must do to meet them there with clarity and confidence, so that early awareness turns into real opportunities instead of stalled intentions.

Trail TIPS
Supporting Awareness With Clarity And Confidence

These prompts help you understand the emotional starting point of your prospects — and your own. Use them to identify whether your firm shows up the right way during this fragile first stage.

What emotional signals are prospects experiencing before they ever reach us?

Does our digital presence help prospects feel safe, not judged?

Do we clearly communicate who we help and how?

Are we supporting Awareness or assuming prospects are already further along?

In what ways could improving this stage create better future growth, such as more inquiries, better fit prospects, or shorter decision cycles?

Trail MARKERS
Supporting The Mindset Of The Prospect

These checkpoints confirm your firm understands the emotional and psychological state prospects are in during Awareness, and whether you're creating an environment that reduces friction instead of adding to it.

- ☐ My firm simplifies information, not complicates it.
- ☐ We communicate in plain, human language prospects understand.
- ☐ We lead conversations with empathy and curiosity, not jargon.
- ☐ We avoid overwhelming prospects with too much too soon.
- ☐ We show up consistently so prospects feel calm, not pressured.

TRAILBLAZING GROWTH
How I Support Advisors At This Stage

Awareness is where clients AND advisors feel the first spark of tension, the moment something is not working, and movement begins.

My role is to help firms understand these emotional triggers and create a presence that meets prospects early and authentically.

During this stage, we identify the moments that wake prospects up — the frustrations, questions, and quiet worries that start the journey. Then we build top-of-funnel messaging and content that speaks directly to those moments, so prospects feel understood long before they reach out.

This is often where better growth begins... not by shouting louder, but by meeting more of the right people at the exact moment they start looking for a guide.

There is a realization point for advisors too, the moment they recognize that DIY marketing is holding them back.

From that point forward, we shift toward clarity, structure, and the support needed to grow with intention, so their own journey mirrors the one they want to design for their best clients.

STAGE 2

EXPLORATION:
WHY PROSPECTS WANDER, LOOP, AND DRIFT

"Sometimes survival means leaving your comfort zone to make your own way."
– Don Connelly

Emotional Outcome: **Clarity**

Exploration is the stage where prospects search for orientation. They aren't choosing yet; they're trying to understand the landscape so they can move toward it with clarity. The better you support this search, the more naturally growth opportunities begin to appear.

Awareness begins the journey, but Exploration is where it becomes real. Once a prospective client acknowledges something needs to change, the next natural step is curiosity. They start gathering information. They compare options. They look for someone they might be able to trust.

Exploration is neither passive nor linear. It's the stage where people try to reduce risk, increase clarity, and understand who can help them. Their goal in Exploration isn't to decide, it's to gain enough clarity to feel safe moving forward.

It's also the stage where most firms lose a large share of prospective clients without ever knowing they existed, which quietly chokes future growth even when everything else looks "busy".

People rarely jump from discomfort to commitment. They step into a wide landscape of possibilities and try to make sense of it. Exploration is where they decide which firms merit more attention and which ones don't.

Firms that understand this stage win early by earning trust long before the first conversation, turning anonymous searchers into warm, growth-ready opportunities.

Across industry research, one theme shows up again and again during Exploration — people rely heavily on subtle trust cues that shape whether they continue down your path or quietly exit.

They are looking for:
- **Clarity** – *"Do they work with people like me?"*
- **Consistency** – *"Do they show up regularly?"*

- **Calmness** – *"Does this feel steady or chaotic?"*
- **Humanity** – *"Do these people seem relatable?"*
- **Proof** – *"Does their experience match my needs?"*

Prospects don't say these filters out loud, but they apply them instantly. Those micro-signals determine whether someone keeps exploring or drifts away, and over time those micro-decisions determine whose pipeline fills and whose does not.

Clients Explore Quietly And Independently

By the time someone lands on your website or follows you on LinkedIn, they've often been thinking about their financial situation for weeks, months, or years. They're searching for guidance without wanting to expose their uncertainty yet. They want to understand their options before involving another person.

They read. They browse. They watch. They compare. And they do it quietly.

They look at different types of advisors and competing firms. They search Google and ask AI for summaries. They ask friends, attorneys, CPAs, or other professionals for names. All of this happens long before they're ready for a meeting with you.

A prospective client in Exploration is not looking for a pitch. They're looking for orientation. Orientation is simply clarity in motion, the process of turning scattered information into a coherent path. They want to understand what the path forward could look like if they choose to take it with you.

Choosing A Route Before You Lace Your Boots

When I prepared for the Inca Trail, I didn't start by booking a guide. I started by learning. I researched routes, checked itineraries, compared tour companies, and read reviews. I looked at the altitude and what the days might feel like. I talked to my adventure buddy to see if he would be interested in joining me. I evaluated gear lists. I wanted to understand the journey before I committed to it.

I was exploring.

Exploration is choosing a direction before taking a step. It's gathering context, eliminating unknowns, and weighing options. Every hiker does this. Every client does too.

Some people want the four-day trail. Others want the shorter route. Others want the views without the work and take the bus. Different motivations. Different capabilities. Different risk thresholds.

Your prospective clients behave the same way. Some want deep planning. Some want focused investment guidance. Some want integrated tax strategy. Some want a full-service relationship. Some want one specific solution.

Exploration is how they discover what feels right and whether your firm feels like the right fit for their long-term growth journey.

Exploration Is Where Most Firms Lose People

Even strong firms fail here. They assume that once someone lands on the website, the hard work is done. They assume the next step is obvious. They assume prospects already know enough to reach out.

The reality is the opposite. Exploration is where people decide whether the path ahead looks safe or confusing.

Most firms lose prospects because:
- their website is unclear
- their message is generic
- their niche is undefined
- their content is inconsistent
- their story is buried
- their differentiators are vague
- their calls to action feel premature
- the design feels dated or overwhelming

Your homepage has to make it crystal clear who you help and what you solve. Research from firms like Gartner suggests that clarity of message can significantly boost conversion rates, even before prospects enter a formal funnel. When advisors niche down and speak directly to a specific client type, visitors feel seen instead of sold.

Confusion kills momentum.

In Exploration, confusion almost always means the prospect leaves and never returns, and those quiet exits add up to years of missed growth.

Exploration Is Nonlinear

Many advisors imagine Exploration as a clean sequence:
Website visit → article → video → contact form → meeting

That isn't how modern clients behave.

Exploration looks chaotic from the outside, but it's simply how people make decisions now. They bounce from Google to LinkedIn to articles to reviews to AI-generated summaries and back again.

McKinsey's research shows that buyers now use more than 10 touchpoints on average before engaging a company, more than double what it was a decade ago. That zigzag pattern isn't a failure of your marketing. It's how confidence is built today.

In practice, Exploration looks like:
- a friend mention
- a Google search
- a quick scan of your homepage
- a LinkedIn visit
- a return visit a week later
- a video watched on mute
- a guide downloaded and skimmed
- a follow on social

People loop. They bounce. They drift. They follow curiosity, not your ideal linear sequence. They gather confidence one piece at a time.

Which is why every touchpoint matters, and why scattered touchpoints create scattered growth.

Exploration Is Emotional AND Logical

Prospects are balancing two forces. Both are active in Exploration. If you speak only to one, you miss half the journey.

Emotion says:
> *I'm overwhelmed.*
> *I want clarity.*
> *I'm scared of being wrong.*
> *I want someone I trust.*

Logic says:
> *Who is qualified?*
> *What is their approach?*
> *What does this cost?*
> *What is included?*

Advisors often assume clients make decisions based on logic alone — comparing features, credentials, or technical capabilities. But behavioral research suggests that a large majority of financial decisions are driven by emotion. If you communicate only to the logical mind and ignore the emotional one, you lose the prospect long before conversion.

Clarity is the bridge between the emotional mind and the logical mind, and Exploration is where that bridge is built. When you understand that Exploration is emotional and intellectual at the same time, you stop marketing as if logic alone will close the gap. And you begin communicating like a guide.

Growth at this stage is not about saying more; it's about saying the right things to both sides of the mind at once.

Digital Body Language — Reading The Clues Prospects Leave

Even though prospects stay silent, they leave a trail of digital behavior that reveals their level of interest. Industry research calls this "digital body language," and it's one of the most overlooked parts of the journey.

A prospect progressing toward trust often:
- returns to your website multiple times
- reads several articles in one sitting
- spends time on the About and Team pages
- watches a video all the way through
- downloads a resource and revisits it later
- follows you on LinkedIn before taking any other step

These actions are quiet but meaningful. They show rising curiosity and early trust long before a prospect reaches out, and they signal where your next wave of growth is likely to come from… if you pay attention.

Advisors Explore Their Marketing Options The Same Way

Your prospective clients explore advisors.
Advisors explore marketing leadership.

Firm leaders ask similar questions:
Who can I trust with our brand?
Who truly understands financial services?
Who can help us grow consistently?
Who won't waste our time or money?
Who will walk with us for the long run?

It's the same psychology. The same fear of getting it wrong. The same desire for clarity and support.

What Firms Must Do During Exploration

Exploration is where your marketing system must work intelligently and consistently. The right assets and experiences quietly guide people from uncertainty toward confidence. Done well, this stage becomes a quiet growth engine rather than a leaky sieve.

Here are the 9 core building blocks:

1. Clarify Your Homepage (and Niche Down)

Your homepage is the front door to your firm. It should immediately speak to the people you serve. The best advisors niche down because clarity builds trust faster than broad promises.

A visitor should know within seconds:
- who you help
- what you specialize in
- why your approach fits their situation

This is where you speak directly to your client avatars. This is where you signal, *"We understand people like you."* A generic homepage makes prospects work too hard. A clear homepage removes the friction and improves the odds that the right people keep moving forward.

Actions to consider:
- ☐ Rewrite your headline to name your audience.
- ☐ Add a clear sub-headline describing the outcome you help create.
- ☐ Add a "Who We Help" section with 3–4 specific profiles.
- ☐ Use client language, not just technical jargon.
- ☐ Include a short welcome video from the founder.

2. Offer A Signature Educational Resource

Most visitors are not ready to talk during Exploration. They want understanding first.

Content Marketing Institute has found that many buyers fully consume at least one piece of long-form content before engaging with a company. Advisors who publish helpful, problem-solving content win Exploration.

Your main call to action (CTA) shouldn't ONLY be "Schedule a Call". Many prospects aren't there yet. Offer education first, then a simple path for those who are ready.

Actions to consider:
- ☐ Create one core resource tied to your niche's biggest need.
- ☐ Use it as your primary homepage CTA.
- ☐ Keep the form simple: name and email are enough.
- ☐ Pair it with a secondary "Talk to Us" CTA for ready prospects.

This resource becomes your trust-building anchor and over time it becomes one of the most reliable drivers of new growth conversations.

3. Build An Automated Nurture Path In Your CRM

Exploration transitions into Evaluation through consistent nurturing. Without automation, prospects drift.

A good CRM can automatically send a short sequence of clear, human messages after someone engages with your content. Without it, warm prospects go cold quietly.

Actions to consider:
- ☐ Use tools like ActiveCampaign or MailChimp.
- ☐ Build a short sequence of 3–5 helpful emails.
- ☐ Include simple stories, videos, and quick wins.
- ☐ Add a gentle CTA at the end of each message.
- ☐ Segment by interest when you can.

This is where the journey becomes connected instead of random, and where growth shifts from sporadic to more predictable.

4. Show Your Face And Your Values

Exploration is emotional. Prospects want to know who you are and what you stand for. They're evaluating character, values, and intent long before they evaluate credentials or process.

Actions to consider:
- [ ] Add real, approachable photos.
- [ ] Rewrite your About page to tell your actual story.
- [ ] Add a "What We Believe" section with 5–7 statements.
- [ ] Feature your team with warm, human bios.

Show that you're more than a logo. People refer and return to firms that feel human... and that humanity fuels long-term, referral-based growth.

5. Make Your Navigation Simple

A visitor should not feel lost or overwhelmed. Clear navigation lowers anxiety and creates flow. When people can easily understand where to go next, they're more likely to keep moving forward.

Actions to consider:
- [ ] Reduce navigation to essentials: About Us, Services, Insights, Contact Us.
- [ ] Add a "Start Here" page.
- [ ] Remove cluttered dropdowns.
- [ ] Make buttons predictable and clear.

Simplicity builds trust, and trust keeps potential growth from leaking out of your site's back door.

6. Publish Consistently On One Channel

Trust is built through consistency. Prospects often watch silently for weeks or months before engaging directly with you. They want to know if you show up regularly.

You don't need to be everywhere. Pick one primary channel and show up reliably and consistently.

Actions to consider:
- [ ] Choose LinkedIn, a blog, or a monthly newsletter.
- [ ] Publish on a steady rhythm.
- [ ] Repurpose content to save time.
- [ ] Lean on a marketing leader to manage the process.

Consistency signals stability, and stability is what long-term growth is built on.

7. Make The First Step Easy And Light

Prospects want a low-pressure way to move forward. They want to explore further without committing too much. A small, safe step reduces friction and builds momentum.

Actions to consider:
- [ ] Offer a short "Fit Call" instead of a heavy consultation.
- [ ] Add a simple "Start Here" button with clear expectations.

- [ ] Record a brief intro video explaining what happens next.
- [ ] Make your calendar link easy to find but not pushy.

Movement should feel safe, because safe first steps lead to more total steps.

8. Create A Calm, Confident Brand Presence

During Exploration, prospects are evaluating your stability. Your brand should feel steady, not frantic. Consistency signals competence and helps people relax into the experience.

Actions to consider:
- [ ] Use clear, calm language.
- [ ] Design with whitespace and clean visuals.
- [ ] Avoid hype or fear-based messaging.
- [ ] Feature testimonials or reviews when compliant.

Your presence sets the emotional tone. AI tools like ChatGPT can help refine language and structure, but your values and point of view still need to lead.

9. Build A Trust Timeline

Every touchpoint in Exploration should move prospects closer to confidence. This stage is about building belief that you are the right partner. Trust rarely forms in a single moment; it compounds through consistent, reassuring experiences over time.

Actions to consider:
- ☐ Map the steps from first visit to scheduling a call.
- ☐ Strengthen weak or confusing points.
- ☐ Ensure message consistency across channels.
- ☐ Keep the emotional experience warm and clear.

When Exploration is done well, Evaluation becomes a natural next step, and your growth curve begins to reflect that smoother handoff.

What Advisors Often Feel During Exploration

Prospects aren't the only ones who feel exposed in this stage. Advisors do too. Exploration brings its own uncertainty — questions about direction, positioning, and whether the path forward will actually work.

Leaders worry:
Will this person be a fit?
Will the prospect be qualified?
Will this turn into a pricing objection?
Will we be compared unfairly to bigger firms?
Will this be a waste of my time?

This quiet anxiety shapes how advisors show up online. Some overcompensate with technical language. Others avoid posting. Others lean too much on credentials instead of clarity.

Just like prospects, advisors want reassurance and a sense of control. Exploration is a two-sided emotional experience, and firms that recognize this communicate with more empathy and confidence, which makes each new conversation feel less like a gamble and more like a step in a healthy growth plan.

Exploration Sets The Stage For Trust

Awareness creates realization of a need.
Exploration creates clarity about the options.
Evaluation creates confidence in the right guide.

Clarity is the prerequisite for confidence, which is why a well-supported Exploration stage makes the next stage feel natural instead of stressful.

When your firm understands and supports Exploration intentionally, prospects arrive at Evaluation already informed, aligned, and halfway toward choosing you, so growth feels less like chasing and more like welcoming the right people at the right time.

In the next chapter, we move into the pivotal stage where trust starts to be built and decisions are made: Evaluation.

Trail TIPS
Making Exploration Easier For Your Prospects

These prompts help you see Exploration from your prospects' point of view and identify where your current experience may be confusing, overwhelming, or incomplete.

If I knew nothing about our firm, what would I think after a 60-second scan of our homepage?

Does our website clearly answer who we serve and what we solve?

Do we offer an educational next step for someone who isn't ready to talk yet?

If a prospect quietly followed us online for 90 days, what consistent story would they see?

Trail MARKERS
Strengthening The Exploration Phase

These checkpoints ensure your firm shows up clearly and helpfully during early research, so curious prospects don't quietly drift away.

- ☐ My firm's website immediately signals who we serve and how we help.
- ☐ We offer educational resources beyond "Schedule a Call".
- ☐ Our social or content presence reinforces our niche and expertise.
- ☐ We use a CRM to track and nurture early-stage leads.
- ☐ We have a clear follow-up path for people who are researching but not ready.
- ☐ We present consistent proof of expertise during Exploration.

TRAILBLAZING GROWTH
How I Support Advisors At This Stage

During Exploration, firms don't need more noise, they need a clearer path. My work at this stage focuses on tightening the experience prospects have while they're quietly evaluating you from a distance.

This is where prospects compare websites, scan LinkedIn profiles, query AI tools, watch short videos, download guides, and research whatever signals they can find online. They're forming impressions long before you ever meet them. So, we shape that path with intention.

I help advisors design the digital breadcrumb trail prospects follow as they research. That includes refining the website, clarifying the homepage, creating the right educational resources, strengthening your Google / SEO / AI search footprint, and ensuring your CRM and nurture paths guide prospects instead of losing them. We also make sure your story, value, and niche stand out in a sea of sameness.

The result is not just a nicer digital presence, but a measurable lift in the number and quality of prospects who arrive at your office door already warmed up, aligned, and ready for a real conversation.

My role is to make it effortless for the right people to find you, understand you, and stay connected while they wander through their options, so that when they finally reach out, they already feel like they know you. At this point, you're not chasing growth anymore, you're receiving it.

STAGE 3

EVALUATION:

WHERE CONFIDENCE BEGINS AND TRUST FINDS A FOOTING

"The most important thing in communication is hearing what isn't said."
– Peter Drucker

Emotional Outcome: **Confidence**

Evaluation is where prospects decide whether your path feels safe, steady, and worth trusting. Your role is to reduce uncertainty and build confidence in choosing you. Confidence at this stage is what quietly converts interest into healthy, repeatable growth.

Evaluation is the stage where the journey becomes real. Prospects have explored their options. They've bounced between websites, referrals, articles, AI searches, and social content. Now they pause to decide who stays in the mix and who quietly drops away.

They're not saying yes yet. They're deciding who even has a chance to earn that yes.

This is where prospects decide whether to:
- keep you on their shortlist
- schedule an initial conversation
- move from curiosity to serious intent
- or drift away and keep walking alone

Evaluation is not about convincing someone. It's about becoming the firm that feels safe, reliable, and aligned while they quietly decide who to trust and where to place their investments.

This isn't a spreadsheet comparison. It's a feeling. Confidence becomes the currency of this stage. Prospects move forward only when they feel grounded, not pressured. When you consistently create that feeling, growth stops being random and starts becoming more predictable.

Edelman's recent Trust Barometer reports that trust is now the single most important factor in choosing a professional services provider — above price, convenience, and features. When your digital presence, messaging, and process feel consistent and intentional, you become the "safe path" in a world where most options still feel risky, and that "safe path" becomes a growth engine competitors can't easily copy.

At this stage, the core question is: *"Do I trust you enough to keep going?"*

The Unspoken Fears Prospects Bring Into Evaluation

Research shows Evaluation is shaped as much by unspoken fears as by logic. Prospects rarely say these out loud, but they feel them:

> *"Will I feel judged?"*
> *"What if I reveal something embarrassing about my finances?"*
> *"Will this advisor pressure me?"*
> *"Will I lose control of my decisions?"*
> *"What if choosing the wrong advisor hurts my family later?"*

These fears are not about fees, performance, or credentials. They're about emotional safety.

Advisors who understand this show up with warmth, patience, and clarity. They lower emotional risk before asking for a financial decision, and that emotional safety is what turns careful evaluators into committed, long-term clients.

The Fork In The Trail

Every hiker knows this moment. You come to a junction with two real choices.

Path 1: Stay on the current trail.
This might mean the prospect stays with their current advisor or continues to DIY their finances. Either way, it's the familiar route, the one you already know. You know its rhythm and its limitations. It hasn't taken you where you want to go yet, but it feels safe because it's known.

Path 2: Take a new trail with a new guide.
This path looks more intentional and aligned with where you want to end up. The guide appears experienced. The markers look clearer. But choosing it requires trust — trust that this guide will lead you somewhere better.

This same fork shows up for everyone in the Evaluation stage.

For clients, it's the choice between staying put or moving toward an advisor who feels more aligned.

For advisors, it's the decision to keep doing what they've always done OR try a new approach / partner / strategy that feels promising but unfamiliar.

At this point, everyone wants the same thing: confidence. Confidence that they won't waste time, money, or emotional energy choosing the wrong path.

How you guide someone through this fork determines what happens next. Done well, it creates momentum and trust. Done poorly, people hesitate and stay exactly where they are.

Evaluation isn't about pressure or persuasion. It's about helping people feel steady enough to move forward — through clarity, consistency, and human connection.

Evaluation Is A Filter, Not A Comparison Chart

Advisors often assume prospects are comparing firms like appliances — fees, services, planning process, differentiators.

That's not how people decide in high-trust industries. Evaluation is a filtering process.

Prospects eliminate firms quickly when they sense:
- confusion
- inconsistency
- lack of clarity
- uncertain expertise
- a missing process
- a generic message
- rushed or pressured tone

Only a few firms make it through that filter.

Evaluation is emotional before it's logical. Prospects want to feel that you understand people like them, that you have a plan, and that you've walked this road before. Clarity may get you into the consideration set, but confidence is what keeps you there and ultimately determines whose pipeline fills up and whose does not.

You don't win Evaluation by shouting louder or sharing more data. You win by creating confidence that makes the client's decision feel simple instead of risky.

Decision Simplicity — The Hidden Advantage

Across the research, one pattern stands out: buyers choose the firm that makes the decision feel simple. McKinsey calls this "decision simplicity", and it's one of the strongest predictors of conversion in professional services because simple decisions get made and complex ones get postponed.

Decision simplicity is created when a prospect feels:
> *"I understand what will happen next."*
> *"I understand what's expected of me."*
> *"I understand how this firm works."*
> *"I understand what problems they solve."*

When the path feels simple, trust rises. When the path feels complicated, trust collapses.

Evaluation is not won by more information. It's won by clearer information, and that clarity is what translates directly into higher conversion, better-fit clients, and healthier growth over time.

Evaluation Is Quiet But Intentional

Prospects don't announce they're in Evaluation. They don't tell you they're re-reading your articles at night, or rewatching a video, or clicking back to your homepage for the fourth time.

You might see some of this with your tech stack, but broadly… Evaluation is silent and intentional.

This is when prospects look for:

- your process
- your story
- your planning philosophy and values
- your experience with people like them
- your clarity and professionalism
- your communication style
- your consistency across channels

The firm that clearly communicates these elements wins this stage and sees that win show up in more right-fit meetings and better close rates, not just nicer branding.

The Psychology Of Evaluation

Three key psychological drivers shape the final decision:

- **Risk Avoidance**
  People want to avoid making a mistake more than they want to make the perfect decision. They look for signs of safety and search for proof they won't regret choosing you.

- **Desire For Confidence**
  Prospects want to believe you've guided others through similar situations. They're looking for reassurance that your path is stable and well worn.

- **Fear Of Rework**
  No one wants to choose the wrong advisor and start over. This fear amplifies the importance of clarity, simplicity, and professionalism.

When you understand these drivers, you can communicate in a way that reduces doubt and increases confidence. Those small reductions in doubt compound into meaningful growth across dozens or hundreds of decisions over time.

How Firms Should Show Up During Evaluation

This stage is where the right assets and signals make all the difference. Below are the 12 core elements every firm should have in place so that your emotional understanding of the client journey is reflected in tangible, growth-driving touchpoints.

1. Showcase A Clear And Simple Process

Prospects need to see that you have a structured way of guiding them. They want to picture the journey before committing. People won't choose a guide if they can't visualize the path.

A 3- or 4-step process usually works best: Discovery, Planning, Implementation, Ongoing Guidance. Not ten steps. Not complex diagrams. Your process is about building confidence, not showing off internal detail.

Include:
- a simple diagram of your process
- a short explanation of each step
- clear language about what clients can expect
- a "How We Work" or "Our Process" page or section

If you don't define your process, the prospect may assume you don't have one, and unclear process almost always shows up later as slower growth.

2. Demonstrate Niche Expertise Clearly

Evaluation is where clients decide whether they're in the right place. If your niche is fuzzy, they drift.

Niche clarity is a major advantage. When prospects feel like your firm is built for people like them, the emotional leap into trust is much easier and specialization becomes a practical growth strategy, not just a branding choice.

Include:
- specific examples of who you help
- clear statements of your specialization
- case studies that reflect your niche
- stories and analogies that mirror their world

Prospects want to think, *"They work with people like me all the time."*

3. Provide Proof Without Overwhelming

Proof builds trust, but too much proof feels like pressure.

Prospects want evidence that you can guide them, not a wall of information. Research from firms like J.D. Power shows that client satisfaction is driven more by communication quality and advisor clarity than by investment performance alone.

Useful proof elements:
- team bios highlighting relevant experience
- photos that show warmth and professionalism
- selected client review excerpts
- awards or recognitions
- articles or media your team has authored
- Google or directory reviews

Proof works best when it's woven into your story, not dumped onto a page… and when it reinforces a simple narrative about why working with you leads to better outcomes.

4. Create A Central "Evaluation Hub" On Your Website

Many firms scatter trust-building elements across different pages. This makes prospects hunt.

Instead, create one page that consolidates the most important Evaluation signals. You might call it:
- Why Clients Choose Us
- Your Journey With Us
- What Working With Us Looks Like

Include:
- your process
- your values and philosophy
- who you serve
- a few brief stories or examples
- a gentle next step

Make it simple, human, and reassuring so a prospect who lands here feels one step closer to saying yes instead of one click away from leaving.

5. Publish One Or Two Deep "Anchor" Pieces

In Exploration, consistency matters. In Evaluation, depth matters.

Every firm should have one or two long-form pieces — a guide, article, or recorded webinar — that show how you think and solve problems.

These pieces demonstrate:
- expertise
- clarity
- your planning philosophy
- your approach to complex situations

Deep content builds a type of gravitational force that pulls prospects toward you. Prospects who resonate with that content often enter conversations already leaning in your direction, shortening the path to growth.

6. Send A Warm "Thanks For Exploring" Email

Most advisors skip this. It's a missed opportunity.
The first email after someone downloads a resource should feel warm and reassuring, not transactional.

Include:
- a simple thank you
- one helpful insight related to what they downloaded
- a line or two about how you help people in their situation
- a low-pressure next step

This sets the emotional tone for the relationship and begins building the kind of confidence that converts quietly over time.

7. Use A Short Intro Video To Build Confidence

A simple 2-to-4 minute video from the founder or lead advisor helps prospects see your humanity. It reduces fear, builds trust, and signals professionalism.

Keep the video:
- conversational
- warm
- clear about what happens next

It doesn't need Hollywood production — a smartphone works fine — but it should be clean, steady, and well-edited. When prospects see your face and hear your voice, the decision immediately feels safer.

Evaluation is where your face really matters because people grow with people they feel they know.

8. Ensure Your LinkedIn Presence Matches Your Website

Prospects cross-check you. If your website looks polished but your LinkedIn profile is outdated or inconsistent, they lose confidence.

LinkedIn should show:
- consistent positioning
- a clear About Us section
- recent activity or posts
- a friendly, professional photo
- niche clarity

Do this for BOTH your personal profile and your firm page.

For Facebook, focus on keeping your firm page current and keeping your personal account relatively private. You can "friend" clients later if it fits the relationship.

Prospects verify your story across your website, Google listing, LinkedIn, firm social accounts, and even your ADV.

Inconsistency isn't just a branding issue, it's a conversion issue... and, over the long run, a growth issue.

9. Provide A Soft, Simple Invitation To The Next Step

Evaluation is where prospects quietly ask, *"What now?"*

If the next step feels heavy, they stall. Your call to action should be a light invitation.

Examples:
- *"If you'd like to see whether we're a fit, let's schedule a simple alignment call."*
- *"If you're ready for clarity, our first call is short and pressure-free."*

Tone matters more than exact wording, and a gentle tone often leads to more first meetings than any aggressive pitch.

10. Avoid Overloading The Prospect

This is the biggest mistake in Evaluation. Advisors often bolt on too much — dense PDFs, charts, calculators, jargon, long decks. The result? The prospect feels overwhelmed and becomes blind to your message, resulting in no action.

Evaluation is not about volume. It's about clarity. Give prospects what they need to feel confident, and resist the urge to flood them, so they move forward instead of backing away.

11. Value Confirmation — The Final Emotional Filter

Research across Advisor360, Kitces, and XYPN highlights a factor many advisors underestimate: value alignment.

Value confirmation happens when prospects sense that your values align with their own. They want to feel that:

- you see the world similarly
- you prioritize long-term relationships over transactions
- you communicate in a way that feels natural
- you treat their goals with respect
- you care about stewardship, not just sales

Values aren't decoration. They're a decision driver and one of the biggest reasons your best-fit clients stay, grow, and refer.

12. "Fit" Calls And Discovery Meetings

Fit calls and discovery meetings are still part of Evaluation. Most of the time, those early conversations are about deciding whether a working relationship makes sense, not closing a deal on the spot.

Yes, occasionally a hot prospect is ready to say yes immediately. But in most cases, those conversations are still Evaluation, not Conversion.

Where Evaluation Ends And Conversion Begins

In real life, the line between Evaluation and Conversion can feel fuzzy. Sometimes a prospect decides during the discovery meeting. Sometimes in the car afterward. Sometimes three weeks later, after a quiet conversation with a spouse.

The timing varies. The pattern does not.

For this book, think of it this way: Evaluation is everything up to the moment of "yes." Conversion is the moment they actually say "yes" and step onto the trail with you.

Evaluation is, *"I could see myself working with this advisor."* Conversion is, *"I want to start now."*

Confidence is the bridge between those two moments, and that bridge is where so much of your firm's future growth is either won or lost.

Evaluation Is Where Trust Quietly Forms

When a prospect reaches Evaluation, they're no longer asking, *"What do you do?"*

They're asking: *"Can I trust you to guide me without having to double back later?"*

Every element of your marketing, content, process, and presence should answer that question.

Your job is not to sell; your job is to guide. Your job is to help the prospect choose the right path, and to show them you're the experienced guide who knows the terrain.

If you communicate this clearly, the next stage becomes possible: Conversion. That's where we're headed next. It's where confident decisions begin to show up as real, measurable growth.

Trail TIPS
Guiding Prospects Through Evaluation With Confidence

These prompts help you see Evaluation from your prospect's perspective and identify where your current experience either builds trust or quietly erodes it.

If I were a prospect, what would I see when I try to understand how we work?

Is our process simple enough that someone could repeat it back after one read or one slide?

Do our website, LinkedIn, and emails tell the same story about who we are and who we serve?

Where might we be overwhelming prospects with information instead of guiding them?

What proof do we offer that we've helped people like them before?

Trail MARKERS
Winning The Evaluation Stage

These checkpoints confirm your firm inspires confidence during this critical decision stage.

- ☐ Our process is simple, visual, and easy to understand.
- ☐ We make our niche unmistakably clear across all major channels.
- ☐ We publish at least one or two depth pieces that show how we think.
- ☐ We showcase team bios, values, and planning philosophy in a human way.
- ☐ Our digital presence — website, social, video, search — is aligned and current.
- ☐ We offer a gentle next step rather than a heavy commitment.

TRAILBLAZING GROWTH
How I Support Advisors At This Stage

Evaluation is where scattered impressions turn into a final judgment. At this stage, prospects are no longer browsing, they're comparing, validating, and eliminating.

My work is to tighten every signal that shapes that judgment, so your firm feels steady, clear, and trustworthy at precisely the moment growth is on the line.

Prospects are cross-checking everything: your website, your LinkedIn, your client experience pages, your niche positioning, your process visuals, even your tone of voice.

They're deciding who feels competent, who feels aligned, and who feels like the safest pair of hands for their future.

I help firms refine the confidence-building elements prospects rely on. We clarify things like your "Why Us" or "How We Work" page, strengthen your intro video, sharpen your process visuals, and tighten your early email touches.

We also align every outward-facing narrative, so prospects don't encounter mixed messages during their research.

My goal is to make your firm feel calm, credible, and aligned at the exact moment prospects are making their shortlist, so choosing you feels like the natural, low-risk decision and your pipeline, conversions, and long-term growth reflect that.

CONVERSION:

THE MOMENT A PROSPECT HANDS YOU THEIR GEAR

"Time is more valuable than money.
You can get more money,
but you cannot get more time."
– Jim Rohn

Emotional Outcome: **Confidence**

Conversion is the moment a client feels confident enough in you, your process, and your path to start building towards complete trust in you as their guide. It's also the moment a relationship shifts from possibility to partnership, the kind of shift that strengthens every mile ahead.

Conversion is often misunderstood. Most firms think it's the moment a prospect signs paperwork or transfers assets. But Conversion actually happens a little earlier, in the instant a person decides: *"I trust you enough to take the first real step with you."*

Sometimes that decision happens during a meeting. Sometimes it happens around a kitchen table later that night. Sometimes it happens days after a quiet conversation on a car ride home after meeting with you.

Here's what surprises most advisors: many prospects have already shaped their decision long before they ever walk into your office.

A recent Wealthtender study found that most people contact 2-3 advisors before deciding and expect the entire evaluation process to take 2-4 weeks. Nearly all of them do extensive online research before reaching out.

The timing shifts, but the essence holds: the meeting doesn't create the decision, it confirms it. By the time Conversion happens, confidence has been gathering quietly, and what surfaces now is trust solid enough to act on.

A prospect in this stage is not casually browsing. They are on the edge of a decision, balancing logic with emotion, fear with hope, independence with relief.

A prospect at this stage has already done the emotional work of Awareness, Exploration, and Evaluation. Now they stand at the trailhead with you, gear in hand, asking: *"Are you the guide I want to trust with the miles ahead?"*

Conversion is not a transaction. It's a transfer of trust. And because trust deepens here, this moment becomes one of the strongest predictors of long-term relationship strength, and with it, long-term firm growth.

The Silent Decision-Maker Most Advisors Forget: The Spouse Or Partner

Across Vanguard, Cerulli, and Morningstar research, one dynamic consistently shapes conversion: the influence of the spouse or partner. Even if one partner leads the conversation, both are deciding.

Partners want to feel:
- respected as an equal
- heard without judgment
- not sidelined
- safe asking "basic" questions
- confident the relationship will feel collaborative

Advisors who ignore the spouse lose conversions quietly. Advisors who speak to both earn trust faster and remove a hidden emotional barrier to "yes." That early sense of shared trust becomes the foundation for a relationship that grows with both partners, not just one.

Two Primary Prospect Types At The Conversion Stage

1. The DIYer Who Reached Their Limit

These prospects arrive with spreadsheets, partial plans, mismatched accounts, or lingering uncertainty. They're intelligent and resourceful... but tired.

Their inner dialogue:
> *"I thought I could figure this out."*
> *"What if I missed something important?"*
> *"I just don't want to feel judged."*

DIYers convert when:
- complexity reaches a breaking point
- the emotional burden becomes too heavy
- the time cost becomes too painful
- they realize a guide will take them farther with less stress

DIYers often feel quietly embarrassed, believing they "should" have figured this out alone. When you normalize that feeling and acknowledge the work they've already done, the tension dissolves.

Their dominant emotion? Relief... if you make them feel respected, not corrected. And relief is often the first emotional foothold that allows trust — and the relationship — to grow.

2. The Client Switching From Another Advisor

Switchers are more emotionally delicate. Cerulli reports that 41% of clients feel guilty or anxious leaving their advisor, even when unhappy.

They're not just evaluating you; they're wrestling with:
- loyalty and guilt
- fear of change
- disappointment
- fear of a lateral move
- transition hassles

Switchers convert when:
- the transfer feels simple
- their past decisions are honored, not criticized
- you show more structure, clarity, and proactivity
- the emotional transition feels safe

Their dominant emotion? Cautious hope. By creating a judgment-free path forward, hope begins to spring and opens the door to deeper engagement. Deeper engagement then creates long-term relationship value for both sides.

The Shared Emotional Drivers

Regardless of whether someone is a DIYer or switcher, both want:
- emotional safety
- process clarity
- simplicity

- reassurance
- a steady guide
- relief from carrying their financial "pack" alone

According to Vanguard's Advisor Client Study, emotional support is the top value clients say they receive from their advisor — not financial returns, not planning tools, not tax projections.

When clients feel emotionally safe, the decision becomes natural, and long-term loyalty becomes possible. Loyalty is the true engine of sustainable advisory-firm growth.

People don't convert because the plan is perfect. They convert because the relationship feels right.

Handing Gear To The Guide

At the end of a long hike, your pack feels heavier than ever. On a 28-mile one-day hike in the Appalachian foothills, my legs were shot. At the final aid station, the guides offered to take my pack. I said no — not because it was wise, but because of ego.

That moment taught me something: People often carry weight alone far longer than they should, even when help is standing right beside them.

Your prospects are no different. They carry:
- confusion
- tax stress
- investment fear

- family obligations
- regrets
- future anxiety

Conversion is simply the moment they stop carrying it alone. Your job is to make handing over their "gear" feel safe, respectful, and earned.

Once they hand you that gear, you begin walking together — a shared journey that naturally deepens trust and strengthens the relationship's long-term value.

The Hidden Barrier: Transition Cost Clarity

One of the biggest blockers to Conversion is not fees, investment strategy, or planning complexity… it's the fear of transition.

Prospects quietly wonder:
"Will this be a hassle?"
"How long will this take?"
"Will transfers trigger tax issues?"
"Will my current advisor be upset?"
"Will I get buried in paperwork?"

Conversion increases dramatically when you:
- outline the transition in plain language
- show the steps visually
- explain what your team handles
- give realistic timelines
- reassure them about typical scenarios

When the transition feels simple, the decision feels safe. Safe decisions are the ones clients stay committed to over time.

What Advisors Should Do During Conversion

Conversion improves when you remove friction and amplify clarity. Here is the 10-step advisor-ready playbook that makes saying yes feel natural, not pressured.

1. Support The Decision After The Meeting

People almost never make a major financial decision in the meeting. They decide:
- on the drive home
- in conversation with their spouse
- rereading your website
- comparing impressions
- asking AI for a summary
- reflecting before bed

Your job is to support that reflection through clarity, not pressure. This is where quiet confidence becomes forward motion.

You help the prospect resolve their tension by:
- sending a warm, reflective "decision support" email
- summarizing their goals in their own language
- restating the path clearly
- confirming that next steps are simple
- reducing uncertainty
- reassuring them that they're in control of the timing

This is not persuasion. This is guidance.

2. Use A "Decision Support Email" To Reinforce Clarity

Send it within 24 hours. Clarity accelerates conversion. The CFA Institute reports that clients are far more likely to hire an advisor who presents their process, fees, and expectations clearly. Conversion is not a comparison of expertise; it's a comparison of clarity.

The decision support email should:
- thank them
- reflect what you heard in their own words
- restate the path forward
- remove ambiguity
- offer a gentle next step to move forward

Clarity lights the path. Confusion makes people turn back.

3. Offer A Light Planning Sample Or Expectations Preview

Examples:
- a one-page plan snapshot
- a visual planning timeline
- a "What Happens First" guide
- a graphic of your 90-day process

People don't commit to what they can't visualize.

4. Make Pricing Simple And Predictable

Pricing confusion is one of the biggest conversion killers. Your pricing communication should be:
- plain-language
- transparent
- easy to repeat
- tied to clarity and outcomes

Calm explanations convert better than technical justifications.

Predictability builds trust, and trust builds durable relationships.

5. Use Identity-Safe Communication

Behavioral research from the Financial Planning Association and eMoney highlights a powerful insight: people convert when they feel their identity is safe.

This means:
- no judgment
- no shaming
- no criticism of past decisions
- no jargon meant to impress
- validation of their existing efforts
- collaborative framing

Identity safety reduces defensiveness, allowing trust (and the relationship) to expand.

6. Use Gentle, Human Calls To Action

Nothing aggressive. Nothing pushy.

Examples:
> *"If the timing feels right, I'm happy to guide you through the next step."*
> *"Whenever you're ready, we can begin the planning process."*
> *"I'm here if you want help deciding what comes next."*

You're a guide, not a closer. Gentle guidance encourages movement without creating pressure, reinforcing a relationship dynamic that grows naturally over time.

7. Provide A 'Welcome Packet Preview'

This single asset can dramatically improve conversion.

Your preview might include:
- onboarding timeline
- who they'll work with
- the first 30 days
- communication rhythms
- documents needed

It transforms onboarding from "unknown" to "prepared."

A clear preview reduces uncertainty and increases readiness — two factors shown to improve both conversion and long-term engagement.

8. Assume They Are Cross-Checking You Everywhere

Prospects quietly consult:
- Google reviews
- your ADV (AUM, fees, disclosures)
- LinkedIn
- YouTube
- their accountant or attorney
- ChatGPT / Gemini ("Summarize this advisor…")
- your blog or articles
- your social media tone
- your website (usually 3–7 revisits)

You must assume they are doing this and you need to ensure consistency across channels.

Consistency across channels demonstrates maturity and reliability, qualities that deepen trust and support long-term growth.

9. Follow A Light, Predictable Follow-Up Cadence

Respectful. Steady. Human.
- Day 1 → Decision Support email
- Day 3–5 → Helpful resource
- Day 7–10 → Warm check-in
- Day 14–21 → Light "here if you need me" message

Not pushy, just present. Consistency signals steadiness, and steadiness is what relationships grow on.

10. Avoid The Three Conversion Killers

- talking too much
- overcomplicating the path
- creating pressure

Conversion is a clarity game. People commit to calm. Calm wins early trust, and early trust compounds into loyalty.

Conversion Is The Emotional Hinge

Conversion is the moment the solo hiker decides it's time to trust a guide. The terrain ahead may look steep. The pack feels heavy. The stakes feel real.

But when the right guide stands beside them — steady, calm, prepared — the decision becomes a quiet yes. A shift from carrying everything alone to sharing the load with someone who knows the way.

Done well, Conversion sends clients into Onboarding with rising confidence instead of second-guessing.

That rising confidence becomes the first building block of a relationship that grows stronger every quarter, every review meeting, every shared win.

Trail TIPS
Helping Prospects Step Into Commitment Comfortably

Use these prompts to examine whether your current process helps prospects feel safe and clearly supported at the moment they decide.

Would a nervous spouse feel included and respected in our process?

Is our transition process simple enough to reduce hesitation?

Do we confirm the prospect's goals in their language?

Is our decision support email warm, clear, and concise?

Does our pricing explanation reduce anxiety instead of creating it?

Trail MARKERS
Guiding The Conversion Moment

These checkpoints ensure your firm provides the simplicity, clarity, and reassurance prospects need to take the first shared step.

- ☐ We send a warm, clear decision support email within 24 hours.
- ☐ We summarize the prospect's goals in their own words.
- ☐ We share onboarding previews to reduce uncertainty.

- [ ] We explain fees in simple, transparent, predictable terms.
- [ ] We use gentle, human calls to action — never pressure.
- [ ] We follow a consistent, respectful follow-up cadence.

TRAILBLAZING GROWTH
How I Support Advisors At This Stage

Conversion is where clarity, consistency, and emotional intelligence matter most. Prospects aren't just deciding on an advisor, they're deciding whether they feel safe taking the first real step. My work at this stage is to build the signals and systems that make their "yes" feel natural and low-risk.

Behind the scenes, this is where I help advisors refine their messaging, simplify process maps, craft Decision Support emails, design gentle calls to action, preview the onboarding experience, clarify pricing, and build follow-up cadences that feel warm, confident, and pressure-free. We also tighten the meeting structure so prospects know exactly what will happen and what comes next.

My role is to ensure this stage feels calm, clear, and trustworthy — never salesy — so the client's "yes" feels earned, aligned, and easy... and becomes the foundation for a long-term relationship that contributes meaningfully to the firm's overall growth trajectory.

ONBOARDING:

BUILDING TRUST AND MOMENTUM

*"Real financial planning is about giving people confidence
in their decisions, not predicting the future."*
– Carl Richards

Emotional Outcome: **Confidence**

Onboarding transforms a client's "yes" into reassurance — the
moment confidence begins to deepen and trust becomes
tangible — and the moment where long-term loyalty, referrals,
and lifetime relationship value first start to take shape.

Onboarding is where the journey stops being imagined and becomes real. It's the moment a prospect becomes a client, hands you the weight they've been carrying, and begins walking the trail with someone instead of alone.

This is one of the most defining stretches of the entire relationship. J.D. Power reports that the first 90 days of the client–advisor relationship have the highest impact on long-term loyalty.

When onboarding feels organized, warm, and well-structured, clients breathe easier. They feel reassured in their decision. They sense momentum.

When those first 90 days feel scattered or silent, growth suffers quietly later in the relationship — fewer referrals, slower wallet share, weaker retention.

Clients enter onboarding with mixed emotions — hope, relief, vulnerability, and nervousness. They've taken action, but they don't yet know the terrain ahead.

Money is personal, tied to identity and aspiration, and the first steps often feel fragile. Your onboarding process must meet that emotional reality head-on. Think of it as the trail briefing before a major hike. The hikers have already committed. Now they need clarity, structure, and confidence in their guide.

Onboarding isn't paperwork. It's momentum building, and momentum, properly created, becomes loyalty... fueling the kind of stable, compounding growth most advisory firms say they want but rarely design for on purpose.

The Client Mindset During Onboarding

Behind every new client is a quiet list of worries they may never say out loud:

"I hope I didn't wait too long."
"I don't want to feel judged."
"I'm worried I'll forget something."
"I hope this isn't overwhelming."

Even affluent clients carry these insecurities. Money touches identity — who they are, who they want to become, and what they fear losing. A strong onboarding experience transforms those insecurities into confidence, turning an abstract "new relationship" into something they can actually trust and grow with.

What clients want most at this stage is simple:

- Clarity – *"Tell me what's happening."*
- Reassurance – *"Help me believe I made the right choice."*
- Structure — *"Show me the plan."*

Silence is the enemy of trust. YCharts found that 67% of clients would consider leaving an advisor due to poor communication. This is why onboarding should feel like a guided hike — steady, proactive, and human — not robotic or transactional.

Clients don't become loyal because of your credentials or tools. They become loyal because onboarding feels safe, calm, and clear. And loyalty, not just acquisition, is what ultimately drives firm growth.

Emotional Checkpoints In The First 90 Days

One of the easiest ways to lower anxiety is to intentionally check in over the first 90 days with a new client, asking questions such as:

"How are you feeling about the process so far?"
"Anything still feel unclear or heavy?"
"Any worries you haven't mentioned yet?"

These small pauses have an outsized impact. Clients remember being seen, not just being serviced. Those moments of being seen are also the early seeds of future advocacy and referrals.

Building A World-Class Onboarding Experience

A powerful onboarding process blends structure with empathy. It establishes a repeatable system that still feels human. Below are practical, deeply actionable tactics you can put into practice immediately.

These are the same kinds of systems I help firms implement when we work together so that onboarding becomes a reliable growth lever, not just an operational step.

1. Use A Simple, Human-Sounding Welcome Packet

A welcome packet is early orientation, the answer to *"What happens now?"* before the client must ask. It should sound like you, not compliance. Clarity matters more than design.

Include:
- a warm welcome letter
- a clear 30-60-90-day roadmap
- a simple "what we handle vs. what you handle" chart
- team introductions with photos
- communication expectations
- portal access and instructions

The packet gives clients something grounding and tangible and signals immediately that your firm runs on process, not improvisation — a subtle but powerful growth signal.

2. Run A Structured Kickoff Meeting (Your Trail Briefing)

This is where trust deepens. Clients arrive hopeful but uncertain. A steady, well-organized kickoff meeting turns that uncertainty into direction. Make sure you include:
- a warm check-in
- the agenda
- a recap of what they've told you
- your planning process
- the 90-day plan
- communication rhythm
- responsibilities and next steps

Visuals help tremendously. A simple map of your process reduces confusion fast and gives clients a mental framework they can repeat to spouses, friends, and future referral conversations.

3. Bring Spouses And Key Professionals In Early

Clients feel more stable when the right people are aligned. Spouses, accountants, and attorneys should be looped in early when appropriate. It reduces their stress and helps decisions flow more smoothly.

This small step does three things:
- shows respect for the family system
- reduces the client's coordination burden
- builds a foundation for smoother decisions later

It also strengthens the relationship beyond a single individual, which is critical for relationship longevity and multi-generational growth.

4. Use AI-Assisted Notetaking To Stay Present

Listening well is one of the most powerful trust builders you have. But taking accurate notes while maintaining eye contact and presence is challenging. AI notetaking tools allow you to be fully engaged while still capturing every detail.

These tools do much more than transcribe. They highlight key points, pull out action items, sync with your CRM, and help you prepare follow-up summaries quickly. They become the backbone of consistent meeting documentation.

AI notetaking tools can help you:
- stay engaged and attentive
- capture key themes and decisions
- auto-generate CRM-ready summaries

- identify follow-up tasks instantly
- reduce administrative time after meetings

You still add the warmth, the empathy, and the interpretation. AI simply handles the administrative burden so your time and energy can stay focused on the relationship.

5. Use Your CRM As Your Onboarding Command Center

Modern clients expect a smooth, organized process. According to Schwab, digital onboarding reduces paperwork errors by nearly 50% and speeds onboarding by 30%.

Use your CRM to drive:
- task lists
- workflows
- reminders
- document tracking
- templates
- progress dashboards

Your CRM becomes the trail marker system that makes a growing client base feel manageable instead of chaotic.

6. Automate A Three-Part Welcome Email Series

Clients are most anxious during the first week. A warm, automated sequence provides structure and reassurance:
- welcome + gratitude + next steps
- first 30 days overview
- kickoff prep

This sequence prevents clients from feeling "in limbo" and reduces the number of clarifying questions they need to ask. Automation done well feels professional, not impersonal.

This automation also allows you to consistently deliver a high-touch experience as you grow, without burning out your team.

7. Create A Shared Checklist Or Portal

Clients often stress about forgetting something or doing something incorrectly. A shared checklist or client portal reduces that stress instantly by giving them visibility into what's complete, what's pending, and what's coming next.

Humans feel calmer when they see progress. A checklist makes the journey tangible. It also eliminates many back-and-forth emails and reduces client anxiety.

A visible sense of progress early on makes clients far more likely to stay engaged and deepen the relationship over time.

8. Use Scheduling Tools To Reduce Friction

Clients love convenience. Scheduling tools eliminate the back-and-forth and communicate professionalism from day one.

Smart scheduling includes:
- buffer time between meetings
- no same-day bookings
- built-in reminders

- personalized confirmation pages
- pre-meeting instructions

Clients love it because it replaces friction with convenience. Frictionless logistics are small on the surface but huge in how "easy" it feels to work with you. People stay with (and refer) advisors who feel easy to work with.

9. Use Short "Loom" Videos For Clarity

Certain onboarding steps — account transfers, portal navigation, document prep — are easier to explain with quick videos than long emails. A short Loom video makes the client feel supported and reduces confusion.

Video also adds warmth. It shows your personality. It demonstrates care. It makes the client feel like they're receiving white-glove service.

Helpful Loom topics include:
- portal walkthrough
- document upload instructions
- how transfers work
- overview of what's coming in the first 90 days
- personalized recaps after key meetings

A 60-second video can save a dozen emails and create a stronger connection. Those stronger early connections are the ones that later fuel introductions and advocacy.

10. Build Templates To Standardize The Experience

Consistency builds trust. Templates ensure that every client receives the same thoughtful, structured onboarding experience, regardless of who on your team is interacting with them. Templates save time, reduce mistakes, improve clarity, and allow you to personalize communication quickly without reinventing the wheel.

Common templates include:
- kickoff agendas
- meeting summary emails
- document request lists
- portal setup instructions

A firm with good templates feels orderly, dependable, and confident in its process. That consistency is what allows you to scale the experience as you grow.

11. Create A First 90-Day Plan With Visible Wins

The first 90 days are when clients decide if they made the right decision. They want forward movement, clarity, and to feel like their financial life is becoming more organized.

A structured 90-day plan shows clients what to expect and when. It breaks the journey into manageable steps with defined outcomes. And it gives you a roadmap for delivering early wins that build confidence.

A great 90-day plan might look like:
- Days 1–7: orientation, portal setup, kickoff meeting
- Days 7–30: document gathering, initial analysis
- Days 30–60: cash flow, tax, risk, and investment reviews
- Days 60–90: planning presentation, implementation roadmap, early wins

Small early wins are like scenic overlooks on a long hike — they reassure clients that the path is leading somewhere meaningful.

Those small wins also anchor the story clients tell later about why working with you has been valuable, which is exactly how organic growth spreads.

12. Measure The Experience

Most firms treat onboarding as a checklist to get through. The best firms treat it as an experience to refine. That means measuring it.

You can track simple metrics like:
- time from yes to first meeting
- time from yes to full account funding
- number of meetings in the first 90 days
- client satisfaction check-in at day 60

A quick question such as, *"On a scale of 1 to 10, how supported do you feel so far?"* gives you real feedback.

Over time, these small measurements help you spot bottlenecks, improve communication, and turn onboarding into a real competitive advantage.

These measurements also give you a clear link between experience improvements and growth metrics like retention, referrals, and client lifetime value.

The Trail Comes Alive During Onboarding

Onboarding is where clients begin feeling the difference between walking alone and walking with a guide. It's where your structure becomes their confidence. It's where uncertainty becomes direction.

The trail becomes real here. The relationship strengthens and trust begins to compound. When trust compounds, growth follows.

Next up is Servicing, where long-term trust (and long-term value) are built.

Trail TIPS
Early Touchpoints That Build Confidence
In The First 90 Days

The following reflection questions help you fine-tune the emotional and operational experience clients feel after they say yes.

How quickly and clearly do I orient new clients after they commit?

Does our onboarding process reduce anxiety or accidentally create it?

Do clients know exactly what will happen in the first 30, 60, and 90 days?

Are we communicating often enough to prevent silence and uncertainty?

Do clients feel emotionally supported, not just technically onboarded?

Are there early "wow" moments that reinforce they made the right choice?

Trail MARKERS
Strengthening Your First 90 Days

These checkpoints ensure your firm delivers a calm, organized, confidence-building experience after a client says yes.

- ☐ We orient new clients quickly with a clear welcome message or packet.
- ☐ Our kickoff meeting follows a structured agenda and reinforces their goals.
- ☐ We share a 30–60–90-day plan so clients know what's happening and when.

- [ ] We communicate proactively during the first 90 days — no silence or guessing.
- [ ] Clients have access to a checklist, portal, or dashboard showing progress.
- [ ] We intentionally create and celebrate early wins that build confidence and momentum and support long-term loyalty.

TRAILBLAZING GROWTH
How I Support Advisors At This Stage

Onboarding is where trust becomes tangible, which means the details matter more here than anywhere else.

My work at this stage is to help advisors build a structured, warm, repeatable onboarding experience, one that reduces anxiety, accelerates clarity, and sets the foundation for long-term loyalty and durable, relationship-driven growth.

Together we design:
- a clear 30–60–90-day onboarding plan
- welcome packets, checklists, and client portals
- automated early-touch sequences
- systems inside your CRM to ensure nothing slips
- videos, templates, and client-friendly resources

My goal is to turn those first 90 days into a powerful differentiator, an experience that makes clients think, *"This is why we chose them,"* and feel increasingly confident with every step, so your growth is built on loyalty and advocacy, not just new leads.

STAGE 6

SERVICING:

DELIVERING ONGOING VALUE
CLIENTS FEEL, NOT JUST SEE

*"The goal as a company is to have customer service
that is not just the best, but legendary."*
– Sam Walton

Emotional Outcome: **Trust**

Servicing transforms early confidence into steady trust —
the feeling clients have that their advisor is watching over their
financial life with consistency, care, and intention, and the
place where long-term loyalty, retention, and referrals are
quietly earned.

The real work of financial advice begins after Onboarding, where confidence starts to settle and trust begins to take shape in everyday interactions.

The systems, plans, technology, and investment strategy all matter, but only to the extent that clients feel supported, guided, and remembered once the initial excitement fades.

Servicing is where you quietly earn the right to keep the relationship — not through big moments, but through consistent ones. It's where clients experience the difference between a transactional advisor and a long-term guide.

It's also where your growth shifts from new-business dependent to relationship-compounding, as clients stay longer, consolidate assets, and eventually introduce you to others.

This stage isn't glamorous. It doesn't get airtime at conferences or show up in marketing trends. But it is the backbone of retention, referrals, and lifetime value.

Servicing is where you demonstrate what it feels like to walk with a seasoned guide — someone who knows the terrain, anticipates the weather, adjusts the pace, and ensures the journey continues confidently.

Great servicing isn't reactive. It's proactive, intentional, rhythmic, and human. It blends systems with empathy. It turns your ongoing delivery of value into something clients can actually feel. And when clients consistently feel cared for, loyalty becomes a natural byproduct.

YCharts found that the number one reason clients fire their advisor is "lack of proactive communication," outranking fees, performance, or service issues. Servicing is not an administrative phase; it's a relationship phase. You win or lose trust based on the rhythm you maintain.

This stage helps you build that rhythm, the long-term cadence that turns clients into lifelong partners and transforms your existing client base into your most powerful growth engine.

The Emotional Shift In Ongoing Service

Once clients settle in, their emotional needs evolve. They're no longer wondering, *"Did I make the right decision?"* They're wondering:
Will the value continue?
Are we still on track?
How closely is my advisor paying attention?

Clients in the Servicing stage want three things, all of which deepen trust:

1. **Reassurance** – They want confirmation that their plan is working and that you're watching over the details they no longer carry alone.

2. **Proactivity** – Clients feel deeply cared for when you anticipate issues before they arise — tax projections, RMDs, life-stage changes, investment shifts, upcoming planning opportunities.

3. **Rhythm** – Predictable communication makes the relationship relaxing instead of reactive. Humans trust what feels consistent.

Think of this stage as the long middle stretch of a hike. The nerves are gone. The initial burst of energy has settled. Now the client relies on your steadiness more than your brilliance.

Clients don't stay loyal because of investment returns. They stay loyal because of how the relationship feels.

Servicing is where that feeling of loyalty is created and where the emotional case for staying, deepening, and referring is quietly reinforced over and over again.

Moments of Truth During Volatility or Mistakes

The long-term relationship isn't defined by the easy months; it's defined by what you do when something goes wrong or feels uncertain.

Markets wobble. Expectations get misaligned. A task gets missed. A client panics. A news headline triggers fear.

Clients aren't evaluating your perfection. They're evaluating your response.

Small but powerful actions:
- reaching out during volatility before they call
- owning mistakes quickly and clearly
- explaining what happened and what you're doing
- bringing them back to their plan and values
- following up quickly and thoroughly on any tasks

Handled well, these moments accelerate trust. A steady guide in bad weather earns more loyalty than a silent guide in perfect conditions and often becomes the story clients share when someone asks why they work with you.

How To Build A World-Class Servicing System

Advisors often think loyalty comes from "wowing" clients. In reality, loyalty comes from consistency — predictable cadence, timely communication, proactive guidance, and the sense that nothing will slip through the cracks.

Below are 12 steps to a world-class servicing system you can implement immediately, so that your day-to-day operations actively support long-term growth, not just short-term satisfaction.

1. Establish A Clear Meeting Rhythm

Predictable meeting cadences eliminate uncertainty and steadily built trust. J.D. Power reports that meeting with clients at least twice a year dramatically increases trust and retention.

A strong annual rhythm may include:
- quarterly or semiannual check-ins
- annual deep-dive planning meeting
- seasonal meetings tied to tax or year-end planning

Meetings shouldn't simply review performance. They should focus on stories, planning updates, life changes, goals, and forward-looking guidance. And remember, servicing is more than meetings, it's communication between them.

Broadridge reports that 78% of clients prefer a blend of digital and human communication — newsletters, updates, reminders, and short educational touches. A clear rhythm on both fronts makes your value feel continuous instead of episodic, which is key for long-term growth.

2. Use CRM Segmentation To Personalize Value

Not all clients need the same level of servicing. Segmenting allows you to deliver tailored, relevant, efficient support.

Segment your clients by:
- complexity level
- life stage
- tax sensitivity
- communication preferences
- interests and family notes

Segmentation allows you to automate and personalize:
- RMD reminders
- tax projection invites
- educational content
- planning touchpoints
- life-stage-specific guidance

Servicing becomes highly efficient without feeling generic, and your team can support a growing client base without diluting the experience.

3. Proactively Identify Planning Opportunities

The best advisors don't wait for clients to ask for help. They identify opportunities before anyone knows they exist. This is where loyalty deepens, not through fireworks, but through steady, proactive guidance.

Proactive servicing might include:
- annual tax projections
- beneficiary checks
- estate plan reviews
- insurance audits
- charitable strategy updates
- retirement projection refreshes
- cash flow reviews
- college funding updates

Proactivity tells clients, *"I'm thinking about you even when you're not in the room."* Over time, that sense of being watched over is what convinces clients to bring more of their financial life under your care.

4. Build A Client Experience Calendar (CEC)

A CEC creates meaningful, year-round touchpoints that keep clients feeling guided between meetings.

Your Client Experience Calendar should include:
- **Educational touches**: newsletters, market perspective, planning ideas

- **Relationship touches**: birthdays, anniversaries, life events
- **Service touches**: tax reminders, checklists, year-end guides
- **Value recap**: *"Here's the value we delivered this year"*

A CEC transforms you from a vendor into a partner and gives your firm a repeatable, scalable growth rhythm rooted in client care, not campaigns.

5. Include The Household and Next Generation

The relationship is stronger when the entire household feels supported. Simple actions include:
- inviting spouses and adult children to key meetings
- offering financial basics sessions for younger family members
- sharing summaries everyone can understand
- coordinating with family decision-makers

Multi-generational inclusion creates multi-generational loyalty. When the whole household feels included, the relationship becomes deeper and more resilient. You are no longer just "their advisor", you are the family's guide. That's how assets stay with the firm across transitions instead of walking out the door.

6. Communicate With A Warm, Human Voice

Clear, simple communication builds more trust than complex explanations.

Use language like:
"Here's what this means for you."
"Here's what we're watching."
"Here's what happens next."

Avoid jargon. Avoid complexity. Avoid corporate tone.

Warmth builds trust. Clarity builds confidence. Consistency builds loyalty, and all three together create the kind of relationship clients rarely want to leave.

7. Use Checklists To Keep The Team Aligned

Behind every great client experience is an organized team. Checklists ensure nothing is forgotten, no detail is missed, and no client feels neglected.

Create checklists for:
- pre-meeting prep
- post-meeting follow-up
- transfers and onboarding
- annual planning workflows
- quarterly reviews
- RMD tasks
- portfolio rebalancing

Checklists prevent inconsistency — the #1 silent killer of client trust and a major drag on scalable growth.

8. Use Technology To Create A Proactive Experience

Technology should extend your care, not replace it. Used correctly, tech helps you stay ahead of client needs and creates a premium experience without burnout.

Helpful tools include:
- CRM automation
- AI notetaking
- Loom videos
- tax and planning software
- scheduling tools
- email automation

The goal is not to automate the relationship, it's to automate the logistics so you can focus on the relationship and maintain a high level of service even as your client roster grows.

9. Maintain A Strong Review Process

The annual review is the anchor of the relationship. It's where clients reconnect with their goals, see progress, and reprioritize. This meeting should feel comprehensive, grounded, and personal.

A world-class review includes:
- life updates
- plan refresh
- tax adjustments

- investment alignment
- risk review
- estate/charitable guidance
- year-ahead roadmap

End with: *"Here's what we'll be focusing on together next."* That simple framing reinforces partnership and gives clients confidence that there is always a next step you are already thinking about.

10. Deliver "Invisible Value" And Make It Visible

Some of your most valuable work is work clients never see. That's a problem because invisible value doesn't create loyalty unless the client knows it has happened.

Send short, clear notes: *"Quick update — we rebalanced today to keep you aligned with your long-term strategy."*

Examples:
- rebalancing
- tax-loss harvesting
- beneficiary checks
- allocation adjustments
- CPA coordination
- cash balance reviews
- RMD tracking

Small. Human. Reassuring. This is how you connect daily work to perceived value, which is what ultimately protects fees and deepens loyalty.

11. Document Client Preferences

Clients feel cared for when you remember what matters to them.

Use your CRM to track:
- communication preferences
- family details
- interests and hobbies
- preferred meeting time and style
- allergies (important for gifting!)
- life goals

Personal details transform a relationship from professional to trusted and make every interaction feel uniquely tailored, even as the firm grows.

12. Create Simple Feedback Loops

Most firms guess how clients feel; the best firms ask. Servicing becomes stronger when you create simple feedback loops. You don't need long surveys.

Use light-touch prompts:
"How supported do you feel right now, 1–10?"
"What's one thing we could do better?"

This feedback gives you early warning signs, clear improvement opportunities, and language you can use to describe the value you already deliver. It also signals humility. Clients notice when you care enough to ask.

And when you close the loop by acting on that feedback, you reinforce that yours is a relationship worth staying in for the long haul.

Walking With A Seasoned Guide

The Servicing stage is the long stretch of the trail where clients settle into a steady rhythm. The nerves are gone. The trailhead excitement has passed. Now it's about momentum, consistency, and trust.

Clients don't stay because the terrain is easy. They stay because the guide is steady.

And this stage prepares the way for the next one — Loyalty — where trust becomes connection and consistency becomes advocacy and where the growth impact of all your earlier work finally becomes visible.

Trail TIPS
Elevating Your Ongoing Client Experience

These reflection questions help you evaluate the emotional health of your servicing stage.

Do my clients feel guided or do they feel like they need to check on us?

Is our meeting rhythm predictable and clear?

Am I proactively identifying opportunities before clients ask?

Does our communication feel warm, human, and steady?

Does the whole household feel included in key conversations?

Are we delivering invisible value... and telling clients when we do?

Trail MARKERS
Strengthening Ongoing Client Service

These checkpoints confirm clients feel remembered, supported, and guided year-round.

- ☐ My firm has a documented client service calendar.
- ☐ We personalize communication throughout the year.
- ☐ Review meetings follow a consistent, thoughtful structure.
- ☐ Client preferences and life events are tracked in the CRM.
- ☐ We proactively identify planning needs before the client asks.
- ☐ Clients consistently feel remembered and cared for.

TRAILBLAZING GROWTH
How I Support Advisors At This Stage

In the Servicing stage, I help advisors build a consistent, year-round client experience that feels proactive rather than reactive.

Most firms already care deeply about their clients, they just need the systems, rhythms, and communication structures that make that care visible and repeatable at scale.

This often means designing a clear client experience calendar, strengthening CRM workflows, and creating meeting structures, summaries, and proactive planning touchpoints that keep clients feeling informed and supported.

I also help advisors surface the "invisible value" they deliver behind the scenes through simple, human updates that reinforce trust.

My goal is to turn servicing into a steady relationship rhythm clients can feel and rely on. When the experience is intentional, personal, and predictable, loyalty deepens because the relationship feels like a true partnership. And that kind of partnership is what ultimately drives sustainable, referral-rich growth.

STAGE 7

LOYALTY:

THE LONG MILES WHERE TRUST DEEPENS AND RELATIONSHIPS LAST

"People will forget what you said,
people will forget what you did,
but people will never forget
how you made them feel."
– Maya Angelou

Emotional Outcome: **Trust**

Loyalty is where trust matures — the long stretch of the journey where clients feel known, remembered, and supported year after year and where the true economic value of those relationships quietly compounds.

Loyalty is the quiet compounding engine of a thriving advisory firm. While it's tracked through retention and tenure, its real power lives beneath the numbers — in trust, confidence, and the willingness to stay when things get uncomfortable.

Servicing helps clients feel supported in the present. Loyalty makes them want to stay in the future and bring more of their financial life under your care.

According to Cerulli, the average client–advisor relationship lasts 10–14 years. That's an entire season of life. And clients don't stay because everything went perfectly. They stay because they trust you, they feel supported by you, and they believe their life is better with you guiding the way.

Loyalty is less about what advisors do and more about what clients experience. It's the emotional thread that tells clients, year after year: *"You still matter. Your story still matters. Your future is still our priority."*

When that message lands consistently, retention, wallet share, and referrals become natural outcomes, not forced objectives.

McKinsey's recent investor satisfaction report states that the strongest predictor of long-term client retention in professional services is "relationship embeddedness" — the degree to which the client feels personally understood, emotionally safe, and part of a shared journey.

Loyalty, in other words, is not the byproduct of good service. It's the outcome of emotional connection over time and the foundation on which sustainable firm growth rests.

Loyalty forms slowly, then all at once. It begins with confidence, grows through consistency, and strengthens through care during life's most fragile seasons.

And unlike the work of onboarding or servicing, which have clear steps, loyalty is shaped by how the advisor shows up over many years of change. It's less a checklist and more a posture, one that clients can feel, and that your growth numbers eventually reflect.

How Clients Experience Loyalty Over Time

Once clients move past the urgency of onboarding and settle into the rhythm of their plan, their emotional needs shift. They begin looking less for explanations and more for alignment, attention, and continuity.

They're evaluating their advisor through three quiet questions:

"Do they still know me?" – People evolve. Families grow. Careers change. Priorities shift. Loyalty deepens when clients feel their advisor is evolving with them.

"Do they anticipate my needs?" – Clients want to feel guided, not managed. They stay loyal when advisors recognize turning points before the client names them.

"Do they understand the story I'm trying to live?" – A plan is numbers. A life is narrative. The advisors who retain clients longest are the ones who stay connected to that story, not just the financial mechanics.

Loyalty isn't a contract. Loyalty is a feeling. And that feeling becomes the deciding factor when clients ask themselves, *"Do I want to keep walking with this firm for another ten years?"*

Where Loyalty Breaks Down

Loyalty rarely collapses suddenly. It erodes through subtle signals:

- fewer proactive touches
- generic communication
- plans that feel outdated
- advisors who forget key details
- a lack of curiosity about what has changed
- silence during emotionally heavy seasons

According to Fidelity, 41% of clients who leave their advisor say the relationship *"felt stale"*. Not wrong. Not broken. Just stagnant. Loyalty weakens when clients feel like the relationship has stopped growing, even if the portfolio hasn't.

When the emotional connection plateaus, the door quietly opens for another advisor to feel more relevant, more present, and more aligned.

The Hidden Seasons Where Loyalty Is Won

The longest stretches of the advisory journey — the years between major milestones — are where loyalty is really tested. Big events like retirement, selling a business, downsizing, caring for aging parents, or welcoming grandkids often redefine what clients need from you emotionally.

These transitions are loyalty accelerators when advisors:
- slow down the pace
- ask more human questions
- focus on emotional readiness, not just financial readiness
- normalize the client's fears
- offer perspective that connects the plan to the moment

Clients rarely remember the mechanics of these conversations. They remember whether you made them feel steadier. Those are the moments they repeat to friends and family when explaining why they *"could never imagine working with anyone else"*.

The Advisor's Role In The Loyalty Stage

At this stage, your role becomes more than a guide. You become:
- **A translator of life changes** – As clients age into new realities, they need help interpreting what those changes mean financially and emotionally.
- **A stabilizer in uncertain seasons** – Markets move. Laws shift. Family dynamics evolve. Loyalty grows when you remain the calm center.
- **A connector across generations** – Clients stay loyal when their family trusts you, not just when they do.
- **A steward of the long arc** – The best advisors don't just manage money, they shepherd families through decades of decisions.

This deeper role doesn't just protect existing relationships, it expands them, turning a single household into a multi-generational, multi-relationship ecosystem around your firm.

Tactical Frameworks For Deepening Loyalty

Below are systems and strategies written specifically for this stage, distinct from Servicing and rooted in long-term relationship depth that naturally supports lifetime value and advocacy.

1. Build "Life Chapters" Into The Planning Process

Instead of an annual review focused on numbers, anchor the conversation in life transitions:
- newly empty nester
- early retirement
- downsizing
- first grandchild
- health changes
- career plateau or career wind-down

These "life chapter" check-ins turn planning into a living process that grows with the client.

Loyalty deepens when clients feel like their plan evolves with them, not just the markets. When the plan reflects the chapter they're actually living, the relationship feels current instead of historical.

2. Capture The Client's Story And Update It Annually

Most advisors document goals, few document stories. Create a simple narrative file:
- What matters most right now?
- What changed this year?
- What worries emerged?

- What brought joy?
- What do they hope the next chapter looks like?

This "living profile" becomes the emotional backbone of long-term planning. It also ensures your whole team knows the person, not just the portfolio. It's a simple way to keep the relationship personal even as your firm scales and more team members interact with each household.

3. Develop A Continuity And Succession Conversation Strategy

One of the unspoken fears clients hold, especially aging clients, is: *"What happens to us when something happens to you?"*

Loyalty strengthens when you answer this fear directly. A brief annual reminder of your continuity plan communicates stability, preparedness, and care. It reassures clients that their loyalty to you isn't a risk to their future, it's a safeguard.

4. Maintain A Multi-Generational Strategy

True loyalty is generational. Clients stay loyal longest when you guide the people they love.

This includes:
- meeting adult children
- offering "financial basics" education
- sharing condensed summaries for the whole family
- facilitating family meetings when major decisions arise

This isn't about selling. It's about stewarding. The growth shows up later, when assets transition, when heirs need help, and when family members already see you as *"our advisor"*... not just *"my parents' advisor"*.

5. Deliver Meaningful Annual Rituals

Loyalty is reinforced through rituals — predictable moments clients come to expect and appreciate.

Examples of annual rituals:
- annual "Letter to Your Future Self"
- personal milestone recaps
- celebratory notes after big life events
- a yearly summary of "Here's the value we delivered this year"

Rituals turn the relationship into a tradition, and traditions are hard to walk away from. They create emotional gravity that keeps clients anchored to your firm even when other options appear.

Walking The Long Miles Together

Loyalty isn't earned through perfection, it's earned through presence. It's built in quiet seasons, uncertain seasons, transition seasons — anywhere clients need reassurance that someone steady is walking with them.

When clients feel seen, remembered, and guided through the long arc of their life, loyalty becomes the natural outcome.

When your firm becomes part of their story, not just their statement, the relationship stops feeling interchangeable — and so do you.

And from loyalty comes advocacy, the final stage of the journey.

Trail TIPS
Deepening Loyalty Over The Long Miles

Use these reflective questions to ensure your client relationships remain vibrant, aligned, and rooted in genuine care, not just ongoing servicing routines.

Do my clients feel known and understood as their lives evolve?

Am I consistently present during their emotionally significant moments?

Have I communicated continuity and stability in a way that lowers long-term anxiety?

Do I engage their broader family and build relationships across generations?

Are we creating rituals or annual experiences that clients anticipate and appreciate?

Has the client–advisor relationship grown stronger over the past year — and can I point to specific moments that made that happen?

<u>Trail MARKERS</u>
Maintaining Loyalty And Long-Term Value

These checkpoints help confirm your long-term relationships are not only stable but deepening in trust, relevance, and emotional connection as the years progress.

- ☐ My firm tracks client tenure and intentionally works to improve it.
- ☐ We adapt planning and communication to reflect life chapters and transitions.
- ☐ We engage spouses, partners, and family members when appropriate.
- ☐ I communicate continuity and succession clearly and proactively.
- ☐ We deliver personal rituals and meaningful annual touchpoints.
- ☐ My firm stays emotionally present during life's major transitions, so clients never feel like they are facing a new chapter alone.

TRAILBLAZING GROWTH
How I Support Advisors At This Stage

In the Loyalty stage, I help advisors build systems that keep long-term relationships warm, relevant, and emotionally grounded. That includes communication rhythms, annual experience plans, and curated value moments that remind clients they matter long after onboarding and long after the novelty of a new relationship fades.

I also guide firms through the life transitions that define loyalty — retirements, business sales, aging parents, health shifts, inheritances, and career changes. In these seasons, clients aren't evaluating performance, they're evaluating support, clarity, and steadiness.

Beyond the household, I help advisors design loyalty systems across generations, from continuity communication to family meeting structures and simple education for younger heirs.

We also build retention dashboards so firms can spot engagement shifts early and intervene before a once-strong relationship begins to drift.

My goal is to turn loyalty into an intentional, repeatable system, one that deepens trust year after year and positions the firm as a lifelong partner through every chapter of the client's journey.

Growth isn't just about adding new names, but about walking farther with the clients you already serve.

ADVOCACY:

WHEN CLIENTS BECOME AMBASSADORS FOR YOUR FIRM

"If people like you, they'll listen to you.
If they trust you, they'll do business with you.
If they believe in you, they'll refer you."
– Zig Ziglar

Emotional Outcome: **Trust**

Advocacy is the moment trust becomes visible, when clients feel so supported and confident in their journey that they naturally share your name with others and your growth starts to come from the stories they tell, not the campaigns you launch.

Advocacy is the culmination of the entire client journey, the moment when trust matures into something outward-facing. Most advisors treat referrals as a tactic. But referrals are not transactional, they're emotional. Advocacy is loyalty that becomes public.

It's the point where a client stops thinking of you as "our advisor" and starts thinking, *"Someone I care about deserves this same clarity."* When that shift happens, referrals don't need to be forced, asked for awkwardly, or incentivized. They emerge naturally because the relationship has become meaningful enough to talk about.

In the hiking world, every great trail eventually creates ambassadors — hikers who finish the route and immediately start telling others where to camp, how to prepare, and why the journey is worth it. They're not paid to promote the trail. They've been changed by the experience.

Advisory advocacy works the same way: a client experiences relief, confidence, or transformation — and feels compelled to share it. Those stories become the most credible marketing you could ever have.

But here's what most firms overlook: Advocacy is designed upstream. It's the byproduct of shared wins, emotional support, and a relationship that consistently feels personal, not procedural. Advocacy is not an accident. It's an outcome of your entire client experience, the natural overflow of a journey that genuinely works.

The Emotional Trigger Behind Advocacy

Clients don't refer you simply because:
- performance was strong
- the plan was accurate
- the meetings were efficient

Those create satisfaction not advocacy. Advocacy emerges when something emotionally meaningful happens. When a client sees you show up in a way that matters beyond numbers.

These advocacy-shaping moments are often quiet:
- you calmed them during a market fear spiral
- you helped simplify a painful transition
- you reached out before they had to ask
- you remembered something personal and followed up
- you guided them through a major life decision

Clients become ambassadors when they think, *"That meant something. Someone I care about needs this too."*

That emotional imprint, not the spreadsheet, is what gets repeated in conversations with friends, coworkers, and family. If it moved them emotionally, they'll move it forward relationally.

How To View The Client In The Advocacy Stage

By the time clients reach this stage, they're no longer judging whether your process works. They're evaluating what it has done for their life. And when the relationship becomes part of their identity, advocacy follows.

Clients in the Advocacy stage often feel:
- gratitude for clarity
- pride in progress
- relief from earlier burdens
- confidence in your long-term guidance
- trust that the relationship will hold steady in the future

And they begin carrying your story into rooms you're not in:
- their CPA's office
- attorney meetings
- workplace conversations
- family gatherings
- community groups

Advisors who treat Advocacy as "optional" misunderstand how high-trust businesses scale. Cerulli data shows that referrals from existing clients are the fastest-converting and longest-retaining relationships — often joining with 2–3x higher trust than non-referral prospects. Said differently, advocacy doesn't just grow your firm, it grows it with the right kind of relationships.

Advocacy is a growth engine disguised as gratitude.

How Advisors Can Proactively Create Advocacy

Advocacy is not something you "ask for more often." It's something you engineer into the client experience by making your value visible, memorable, and emotionally meaningful so clients feel proud, not pressured, to talk about you.

1. Make Your Value Story Repeatable

Clients don't use industry language. They need straightforward, shareable phrases like:
> *"They helped us simplify everything."*
> *"They guide us through major life transitions."*
> *"They make money decisions feel less stressful."*

You're not scripting clients, you're equipping them with simple, memorable phrases.

Create a digital one-page "Here's Who We Help" client-friendly summary that clients can share when the moment is right. This alone increases advocacy dramatically. It gives clients something concrete to pass along when they're asked, *"Who do you work with?"*

2. Equip Clients With Stories, Not Scripts

People don't refer processes, they refer stories. Seed your conversations with small, anonymized examples so clients can recall them later. These become the narratives they naturally retell.

Give clients stories that are simple, human, and helpful. They will carry those farther than any brochure. Stories travel where sales language never will.

3. Make Referring Emotionally Safe

Clients hesitate when referrals feel risky. Reduce the pressure by saying: *"I'm always happy to be a resource to someone you care about — no expectations. Our first call is always light and helpful."*

This makes the referral feel like offering help, not making a sales introduction. When clients know you won't "pounce" on their friends, they're far more willing to open the door.

4. Create Shareable Content Clients Want To Pass Along

Make content that solves real problems or answers questions people struggle with. Clients will naturally forward it because they want to help someone... and it reflects well on them.

Examples include:
- helpful financial guides
- retirement checklists
- tax deadlines summaries
- charitable giving strategies
- educational videos
- simple visual explainers
- timely market narratives
- family meeting templates

These get forwarded because they feel useful, not promotional. The right content can turn your whole client base into a network of silent marketers. When your ideas are easy to share, your name travels with them.

5. Host Events People Want To Invite Others To

Events create some of the strongest advocacy moments because they give clients a low-risk way to introduce you to people they care about. The key is hosting experiences that feel worth sharing.

Examples include:
- wine tasting
- dinner workshops
- holiday open houses
- charity volunteer days
- market outlook events
- 55+ retirement transition nights
- women's financial wellness sessions
- client appreciation brunches

Clients bring people to events that make them look good. People want to associate with something that feels elevated and thoughtful. The event should feel warm and well-organized. When clients feel proud to bring someone, advocacy becomes effortless. You're not just hosting an event; you're creating a setting where introductions feel natural instead of forced.

6. Strengthen Multi-Generational Advocacy

One of the most overlooked sources of advocacy is a client's own family. Adult children, parents, siblings, and even extended relatives often influence financial decisions.

When you build trust with the entire family system, advocacy expands naturally.

Simple ways to engage families include:
- hosting an annual family meeting to discuss planning themes
- creating a "next generation" workshop on financial basics
- sending relevant content to adult children with permission
- helping aging parents organize documents and beneficiaries

When families see the role you play across generations, you stop being "the advisor" and become the family's guide. And families who feel supported don't just stay, they advocate. They bring you into new chapters and new relationships without you ever having to "pitch."

7. Build Professional Advocacy Wells / Centers Of Influence (COIs)

Accountants, attorneys, insurance professionals, and bankers are all surrounded by people in transition. Equip them with helpful resources and clarity about who you serve.

These partners become strong advocacy wells when you make collaboration easy by:
- sending a quarterly resource
- sharing short planning guides
- offering joint educational events

- making intros proactively
- collaborating on client cases

When COIs trust your expertise and experience your reliability, referrals begin to flow naturally. A handful of well-nurtured COIs can become some of your most consistent advocates.

8. Simplify The Referral Path

Most advisors make referring too difficult. Build easy pathways, such as:
- a "referral page" on your site
- a simple introduction email template clients can forward
- a single "next step" link (15-minute fit call)
- a shareable resource that leads into a conversation
- a QR code at events
- a soft, evergreen line in newsletters *("If someone you know needs clarity... ")*

When the referral friction goes down, the frequency goes up. If it takes more than a few clicks or a short email to connect someone with you, the moment often passes.

When A Client Becomes An Advocate

At this stage, your clients are no longer hikers following your trail, they're storytellers. They've been guided, supported, reassured, and understood. And now they share your name because it feels right, not because they were asked.

Advocacy is pride.
Advocacy is gratitude.
Advocacy is the journey retold.

Firms who consistently create this emotional imprint never need to "chase" growth. Their clients carry the story forward for them. Growth becomes less about pursuit and more about gravity. The right people are pulled in by the experiences others have already had with you.

Trail TIPS
Turning Loyalty Into Advocacy

These questions help you identify the simple, repeatable actions that shift clients from loyalty to active advocacy.

Where can I create small "story moments" clients naturally repeat to others?

How can I make referrals feel emotionally safe, low-pressure, and helpful?

What content or resources could I create that clients would be proud to share?

Which client events or gatherings could naturally encourage guests or introductions?

How can I deepen multi-generational relationships so the entire family becomes an advocacy engine?

What language, stories, or simple phrases are my best clients already using when they describe us — and how can I reinforce those?

Trail MARKERS
Strengthening Your Advocacy Engine

This set of checkpoints helps you confirm your firm is creating experiences worth sharing and making it easy for clients and COIs to advocate for you.

- ☐ My firm equips clients with simple, memorable language to describe what we do.
- ☐ We intentionally create moments that spark stories, not just satisfaction.
- ☐ Our client events are designed to be "bring-a-friend" worthy.
- ☐ We nurture multi-generational ties so advocacy grows beyond one person.
- ☐ My firm maintains strong, reciprocal COI relationships that naturally generate referrals.
- ☐ We make the referral path simple, human, and pressure-free.
- ☐ A meaningful share of new relationships each year comes from existing clients and partners, confirming that advocacy is built into our experience, not bolted on.

TRAILBLAZING GROWTH
How I Support Advisors At This Stage

In the Advocacy stage, I help advisors build structured, repeatable systems that turn loyalty into organic growth. That includes shaping clear referral language, crafting simple "Who We Help" summaries, and designing shareable content and client-friendly stories that make it easy for clients to describe your value with clarity and confidence.

I also help firms design annual experience plans that create natural advocacy moments — thoughtful interactions that make clients feel seen, supported, and proud to introduce you to others. These aren't gimmicks. They're intentional touchpoints that help clients notice and articulate the value they experience all year long.

Beyond the client base, I help advisors deepen their COI networks, build light referral pathways, and create client events that genuinely inspire guests and introductions. When partners and clients understand how to talk about you, advocacy grows effortlessly.

My goal is to engineer advocacy into the rhythm of your client experience so referrals become a natural byproduct of trust, not a sales tactic. Your firm's growth is then powered by the very journey you've designed for the people you serve.

CONCLUSION

Clarity leads to confidence. Confidence leads to trust. Trust leads to transformation — for your clients and for your firm.

Almost every client journey begins the same way.

A prospective client sits at their kitchen table staring at spreadsheets, tax forms, retirement projections, insurance statements, and long-forgotten logins.

They feel the weight of uncertainty, the burden of complexity, and the fear of missing something important. They want clarity but cannot find it. They want support but hope they will not be judged. They want guidance but are not yet ready to ask for it.

Even if they're already working with another advisor, this is where the journey begins. Not with a meeting or a form-fill, but with a quiet moment of realization when someone recognizes they cannot carry the financial weight alone.

And that is the purpose of this book. To show you the path your prospective clients walk long before they ever meet you. To help you become the guide they hope exists. To reveal how clarity opens the door, how confidence carries them forward, and how trust ties the entire relationship together.

Because clients are not searching for more information, they are searching for a guide.

Someone steady. Someone experienced. Someone who can transform uncertainty into clarity, complexity into confidence, and vulnerability into trust.

Marketing is not about persuading. It's about entering the journey early — meeting someone long before they have the courage to ask for help — and walking with them until they feel certain again.

The Journey Is The Differentiator

In a world crowded with advisors, robo platforms, automated tools, and AI-generated noise, the way you guide people is what truly sets you apart.

Not your logo. Not your tagline. Not your fee schedule.

Your differentiator is the clarity of your process, the confidence you inspire, and the trust you build across every stage of the client journey.

That is the experience people remember. That is the experience they talk about. That is the experience they stay for, and the one that fuels meaningful, sustainable growth.

Your Client Is Hiking A Trail They've Never Walked

You have walked these miles hundreds of times. They have not.
You know the terrain. They do not.
You recognize the hesitation. They do not.
You understand how to pace the journey. They do not.
You know how to help them finish.

This is why clients hire advisors — and why firms hire marketing leaders.

Not for quick tactics or one-off campaigns, but for a guided journey that leads to clarity, confidence, and trust.

Everything You Want Is Downstream Of Clarity

Clarity in who you serve.
Clarity in the journey you guide them through.
Clarity in how you communicate.
Clarity in your expectations.
Clarity in their next steps.

Clarity removes uncertainty, creates momentum, and earns confidence.

And confidence, applied consistently, builds trust.

When your process is clear, clients trust the path.
When your communication is clear, clients feel steady.
When your experience is clear, advocacy becomes natural and your growth becomes inevitable.

Clarity is not a luxury. It's the foundation of the modern advisory firm.

This Book Is A Starting Point, Not A Finish Line

You now have the map. The trail markers. The stages. The psychology. The frameworks. The systems. But maps do not create progress — walking does.

You do not need to rebuild your entire journey overnight. You only need to take the next step and then the next and then the next.

The Journey Your Future Clients Are Already On

Somewhere right now a future client is at the beginning of this journey. They are staring at something they do not understand. They are carrying stress they have not admitted out loud. They are hoping clarity will show up.

They will not call this a funnel or a pipeline; they will call it trying to get their life back in order.

And when they finally reach out, they will not remember your slogan or your latest market update. They will remember how they felt the first time your presence crossed their path.

Calmer. Understood. Less alone.

That is the power of clarity.
That is the promise of confidence.
That is the foundation of trust and the beginning of advocacy-fueled growth.

Your Work Creates Ripples

Every advisor I have worked with underestimates the impact of their guidance. You do more than manage money; you change families. You shape transitions. You influence legacies. You create stability during seasons when life feels anything but stable.

And when you guide someone with clarity, confidence, and trust, the effect ripples outward to their spouse, their children, their community, and everyone who depends on them.

This is why the journey matters. This is why the client experience matters.

Not because it grows your firm. But because it strengthens the lives of the people who trust you.

A Final Thought

You do not have to walk your own business-growth journey alone.

Many advisors try to carry all the gear themselves. Marketing, messaging, content, social, events, compliance, client experience, retention. And like any hiker overloaded with weight, they eventually slow down, burn out, or get stuck.

Guides matter in business just as they matter in retirement planning. Someone to lighten the load. Someone to scout the next mile. Someone to help you build a journey worthy of the clients you serve.

And when you're ready for that kind of support, I'm here.

Thank You For Walking This Journey With Me

Thank you for your time and attention. My hope is that this book becomes a trail map you return to often, not just for inspiration but for steps you can put into motion right away.

Your clients need clarity.
Your prospects need guidance.
Your community needs leadership.
Your firm needs a journey worth taking.

And you have everything you need to build it.
Now, go guide!

ACKNOWLEDGMENTS

To my boys, Cooper and Colin, who give me a reason to wake up each day and dream bigger than the day before. Everything I build is ultimately for you. Thank you for inspiring me to be a better man, to create an exceptional life for our family, and to show you through my actions how young men grow into strong, thoughtful adults.

To my mom, the lifelong librarian who filled my childhood with stories, curiosity, and an appreciation for books that would eventually lead me here. Thank you for giving me every advantage I needed to succeed later in life.

To my dad, Dr. Mike Crampton, for showing me what it looks like to pursue advanced education, to pivot boldly when life demands it, and to always place family above everything else. You also gave me the DIY gene, which has served me more times than I can count.

To Dr. Joel Poor, professor at the University of Missouri–Columbia, whose humor, corporate-world stories, and unforgettable Marketing 101 class set me on the path that became my entire career. Thank you for opening that door.

To the colleagues and friends, who encouraged me to write this book, whether through their own examples or through conversations that sparked new ideas. Your influence, even in brief moments, helped push this project from intention to reality.

To my lifelong friend and adventure travel buddy, John Buhr, who brought storytelling into my life long before I ever thought of writing a book. Thank you for the hikes, the conversations, and the unforgettable moments, especially on the Inca Trail.

To my clients, past and present, who allow me to do work I genuinely love. You trust me with your firms, your goals, and your growth, and that trust is what continues to make this work meaningful.

And finally, **to my readers**, for letting me be part of their journey as they grow their firms and become better guides for their clients.

ABOUT THE AUTHOR

Joel Crampton is a strategic marketing leader and the Founder of CMO Alpha, where he serves as a fractional Chief Marketing Officer (CMO) for financial services firms who are seeking clarity, structure, and measurable growth. With more than 20 years of experience in marketing leadership roles — including investment management, insurance, fintech, and professional services — Joel brings a rare combination of industry expertise and cross-functional insight. He holds an MBA in Marketing from the University of Missouri–Kansas City and formerly held his Series 6, Series 63, and multiple insurance licenses.

Joel lives in Kansas City, Missouri with his two sons, Cooper and Colin. Away from the office, he's a dedicated traveler and outdoor adventurer. Completing multi-day hikes, such as the Inca Trail to Machu Picchu, has shaped his belief that every meaningful journey — financial or otherwise — requires a steady guide, thoughtful preparation, and intentional steps forward.